Teddy Bears on Paper

Susan Brown Nicholson

A carefully researched text
and price guide about Teddy Bear
graphics on antique paper items

Published by
Taylor Publishing Company
1550 W. Mockingbird Lane
Dallas, Texas 75221

DEDICATION

This book is affectionately dedicated to my children LORA LEE and JAMES WILLIAM in the International Year of the Teddy Bear 1985.

TEDDY BEARS ON PAPER

A *Collectors'* **SHOWCASE** Library Publication

Produced by
D. Keith Kaonis and *Collectors'* **SHOWCASE** Magazine
San Diego, California

Published by
Taylor Publishing, Dallas, Texas

Author: **Susan Brown Nicholson**
Art Director: **Grace Anne Swanson**
Design: **Grace Anne Swanson**
   Jeremy Crockett
Photography: **D. Keith Kaonis**
Production: **Grace Anne Swanson**
Color Photo Lab: **Diversified Photo**
   San Diego, California
Color Separation: **Mesa Color**
   San Diego, California

Catalog number 741.6NIC

Copyright © 1985 by Susan Brown Nicholson. All Rights Reserved. No part of this book may be reproduced or transmitted in any form or by any means, electronic or mechanical, including photocopying, recording or by any information storage and retrieval system, without permission in writing from the copyright owner.
Manufactured in the United States of America
First Printing, 1985
Library of Congress Number: 85-062975
ISBN 0-917205-03-0

Contents

Introduction 5
Story of Roosevelt 6
Political and Social History 16
Advertising 19
Artist Signed Post Cards 25
Post Card Sets 33
Spirit of the Teddy Bear 57
Novelty Post Cards 73
Real Photo Post Cards 81
Paper Dolls 89
Sheet Music 108
Other Paper Teddies 111
Books 121
Conclusion 125
Index 126

Illustration by R.K. Culver from the book
More About The Roosevelt Bears.

ACKNOWLEDGEMENTS

Any book demands the cooperation and patience of family and friends. I would like to thank the following people for their contributions and encouragement.

My husband, **James Hamilton;** my parents **Martha Jane** and **William Brown;** my sister **Barbara Anne** and my brother - **Edward Allen** for always encouraging me to be me. My children, **Lora Lee** and **James William,** for accepting many of my responsibilities, as well as their own, so this project could be finished. **Bina Nicholson** and **Millie Gode** for always being interested in what I'm doing.

I would like to thank **Lois Pietz** for introducing me to my first post card show. I would like to thank **Dan Miranda** for inspiring my interest in post cards.

Sandy and **John Millns,** post card dealers extraordinary, for helping me put together my collection.

Jan Banneck, for the encouragement, research and loan of her paper dolls.

Rita Nadler for the loan of many exceptional post cards and the courage to work with me on a moments notice till all hours of the night.

Gotham Book Mart owner, **Andreas Brown,** my mentor, for the loan of real photographic and political post cards. A real Teddy Bear hug for you, Andy.

Hal Ottaway, for the loan of exceptional political post cards and always being willing to help when I need him.

James Morrison, for finding one of the rarest post cards in my Teddy Bear collection, but mostly for just being Jim.

Joseph Horemans, European dealer, for supplying me with post cards and books.

Ellen Budd, for her continued intellectual support and her research knowledge.

David Bonomo, a new acquaintance, for the loan of political post cards.

Joseph and **Teresa Miracle,** for the loan of the Busy Bear book and Wall post cards.

Jim Davis, for the loan of a key advertising post card.

Ralph Williams, for the loan of the hold-to-light Santa with Teddy.

Roy Nuhn, for the loan of the Roosevelt Bears in England.

Joan DiGennaro, for the loan of the Roosevelt Bears in Switzerland.

I would also like to extend a special thanks to two sheet music collectors who, even though we have never met, unselfishly loaned me their Teddy Bear sheet music. Thank you **Joseph Albertson** and **Danny Crew.**

Introduction

The purpose of this book is to introduce a variety of Teddy Bear graphics on antique paper items.

There are numerous children's books featuring the Teddy Bear, hundreds of post cards and even songs. He has modeled for many artists and posed for even more photographers.

Today, with the space and money required to collect antique Teddy Bears, many collectors have specialized in collecting two dimensional Teddies on magazine covers, valentines, paper dolls, post cards, books and sheet music.

This book attempts to illustrate a sampling of all important antique paper Teddy Bear items. A wide variety of material was selected to give a comprehensive view of what is available to the collector today. A concentrated effort was made to include all available research on illustrators of Teddy Bears, to picture a variety of complete post card sets and to include a valuable price guide compiled by a panel of knowledgeable dealers.

While some of the items used to illustrate this book are extremely scarce, most are readily available through antique shows, flea markets and post card shows throughout the world.

With this sampling as an incentive we hope you will find many more examples of Teddy Bears or dressed bears emulating people on paper collectibles.

Good luck with your quest.

Story of Roosevelt

Theodore Roosevelt's name became well known in 1898 when he assembled and commanded a group of men known as "Roosevelt's Rough Riders" who fought in the Cuban War. When he returned to the United States, he was made Governor of New York and in 1901 became the Republican Vice-President under William McKinley. Later in that year, when President McKinley was assassinated, Roosevelt became president. That November, an incident occured that was to inspire the creation of the Teddy Bear.

Roosevelt. The Real "Teddy" Bear.

President Roosevelt was visiting the South to settle a boundary dispute between Mississippi and Louisiana and planned to draw a new line between the two states. During a break in negotiations, Roosevelt was invited to go hunting at Smedes on the Mississippi Delta. Several versions of that day have been reported, some say a malnourished bear was driven from the woods for the President to shoot, some say a small sickly bear was tied to a nearby tree for him to shoot, others say it was not a bear but a cub which the President was instructed to shoot. The only certainty is that the President refused to shoot the bear because it was unsportsmanlike.

One of the most famous cartoonists of the day, Clifford K. Berryman, heard of the incident and immortalized it in a cartoon. The cartoon pictured a small bear with a rope around its neck being held by a man in Rough Rider clothing. The President had his back to the bear with his arm outstretched indicating he would not shoot. The caption "Drawing the Line in Mississippi" gave the cartoon a double meaning. After the initial appearance of the Berryman cartoon, the drawing appeared in newspapers throughout the United States.

Even though Roosevelt went on in his Presidency to initiate the work on the Panama Canal, help settle the Russo-Japanese war and to break up monopolies, he is best remembered by millions of people for his link to the Teddy Bear. Neither President Roosevelt nor Clifford Berryman could have realized that they had played such a crucial role in the creation of a childhood institution.

Starting in 1905, readers awaited impatiently for each day's newspaper to follow the latest episode in the lives of Teddy B and Teddy G. For a year their adventures were syndicated through twenty newspapers, followed by the publication of four books based on the serial.

Written by Paul Piper, pen name Seymour Eaton, the Roosevelt Bear books (1906-1908) were immediately successful. From them we learn that the black bear's name was Teddy B for Black or Brown and Teddy G was the Gray bear's name for Gray.

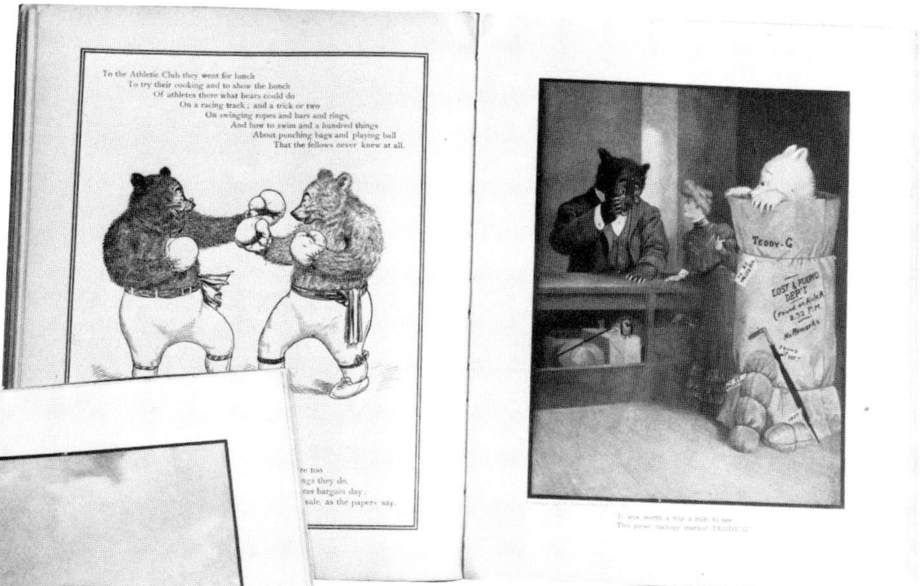

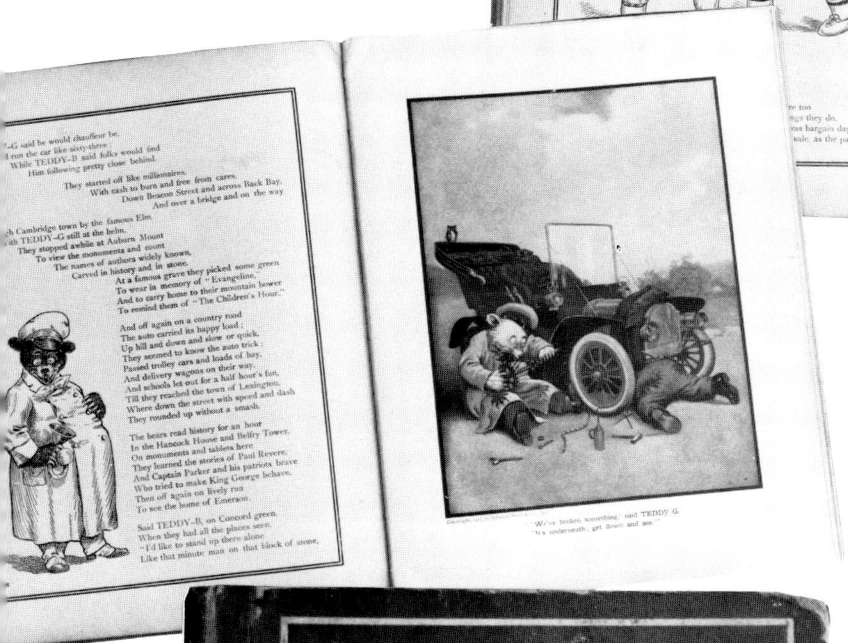

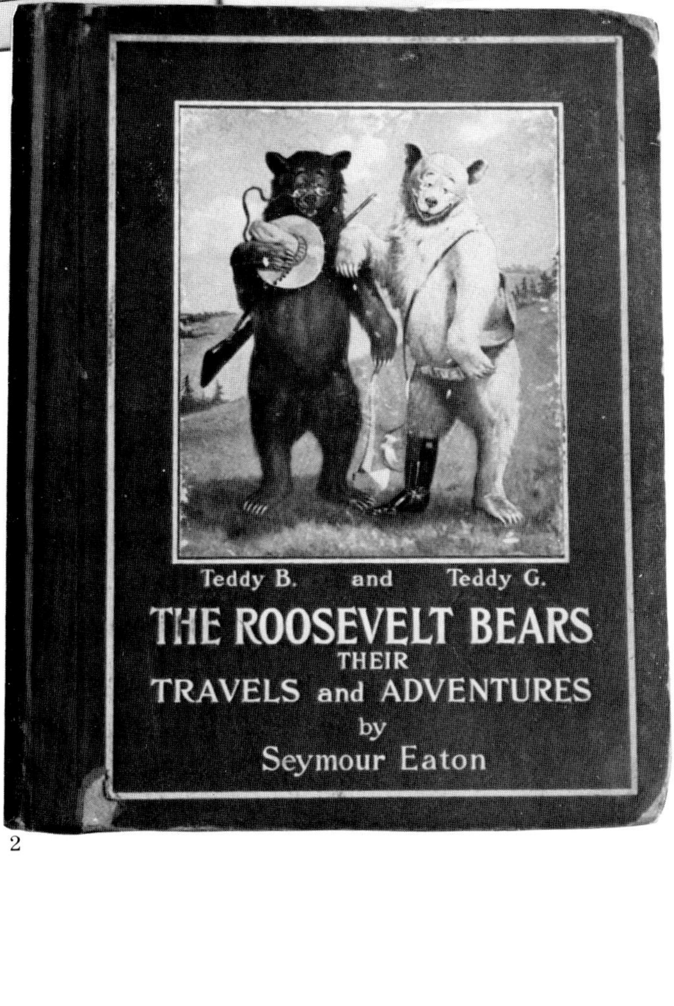

STORY OF ROOSEVELT

The first title in the series was *the Roosevelt Bears — Their Travels and Adventures* containing 180 pages with illustrations by V. Floyd Campbell. The verses described the bears' experiences as they traveled by train from the Rocky Mountains to New York. This book had sixteen color illustrations including frontispiece and cover.

The second book, *More About the Roosevelt Bears*, told of Teddy B and Teddy G's adventures in New York and their trip back to their home in Colorado. In this book, they even met President Roosevelt. This time the illustrations were by R.K. Culver but were similar in style to the first book. This book had sixteen color illustrations.

R.K. Culver also illustrated the third volume entitled *The Roosevelt Bears Abroad*. This adventure took the bears across the Atlantic to England, through Europe and home again by way of Egypt.

The final book in the series was *The Bear Detectives* (1908) in which Paul Piper, pen name Seymour Eaton, had Teddy B and Teddy G solving several nursery rhyme mysteries including finding the tails of Little Bo Peep's sheep. The task of illustration once again changed hands with collaboration by Francis P. Wrightman and William K. Sweeney creating the artwork. With fewer pages than the first three volumes -152 compared to nearly 180 pages each in the other books - this final book also contained only eight color illustrations.

These four books comprise the entire adventures of Teddy B and Teddy G, the Roosevelt Bears. However, there are an additional ten books which are sought after by collectors. The second series were published by Barse and Hopkins beginning in 1915. By 1921, the series of ten books were finished, however, we must remember these were not additional stories but segments of the first four books by Edward Stern and Company, Inc. They had fewer pages, fewer illustrations and sold for 40 cents instead of $1.50, the suggested retail of each for the initial four books.

The ten titles are:

The Traveling Bears in Fairyland
The Adventures of the Traveling Bears
The Traveling Bears in the East and West
The Traveling Bears in New York
The Traveling Bears in Outdoor Sports
The Traveling Bears at Play
The Traveling Bears in England
The Traveling Bears Across the Sea
The Traveling Bears Detectives
The Traveling Bears' Birthday.

4

Another item which features the Roosevelt Bears is a writing tablet. The original Teddy Bear tablets were distributed by G. Sommers in 1907. The ten different designs were taken from the Roosevelt Bear books published by Edward Stern and Company. The size is 6½ inches by 9½ inches (16.51 cm × 24.13 cm) with 100 pages of ruled, newsprint quality paper. The wholesale price was 39 cents a dozen.

Post card publishers immediately responded to the Teddy Bear craze. While not the first cards to be published, the post cards highly sought after today relating to President Roosevelt are the *"Roosevelt Bears"* published by Edward Stern and Company of Philadelphia. In reality Teddy B and Teddy G were represented as friendly but lifesize bears, not the cuddly type teddies we are most familiar with today.

The Roosevelt Bear post cards have been the most confusing to collectors. There are actually four different groups of Roosevelt Bear post cards. The first group is numbered 1-16, the second group is numbered 17-32, the third group is 17-20 with verses but not titles and the fourth group has no numbers but consists of at least five cards.

STORY OF ROOSEVELT 11

The first sixteen post cards, numbered 1-16, produced by E. Stern in 1906, reproduced the illustrations of V. Floyd Campbell in Eaton's *"Teddy B and Teddy G, The Roosevelt Bears — Their Travels and Adventures."* These first sixteen cards have titles on each card.

12 STORY OF ROOSEVELT

In the second set of sixteen post cards, numbered 17-32, the cards were produced from illustrations of *"More About Teddy B and Teddy G, the Roosevelt Bears,"* published in 1907 and illustrated by R.K. Culver. This second set has titles for each card.

37 38

39 40

A third group produced was also numbered 17-20 minus the titles, but with quotes from the book which corresponded to the pictures. Cards 17 and 18 are horizontal images while the other cards are vertical. Cards 17 and 18 are entirely different images from any of the other cards. However, cards 19 and 20 in this grouping of no title cards are identical to images 26 and 27 in the titled group. Any cards numbered 17-32 are harder to find than those numbered 1-16 and command higher prices.

The fourth group is not numbered and are illustrations from the third book, *The Roosevelt Bears Abroad*. This volume was illustrated by R.K. Culver. The five post cards from this group include the bears visiting England, Ireland, Scotland and Switzerland and returning home to shake hands with Uncle Sam.

The last two groups are very elusive and could contain as many as sixteen cards each. However, after considerable research these are the only examples known today.

Political and Social History

The increasing popularity of the Teddy Bear as a stuffed toy and the great success of the Roosevelt Bears in serial, book and post card form led President Roosevelt to adopt the Teddy Bear as his political mascot. Many political fund raisers, general meetings and the Republican convention used the Teddy Bear for a standard decoration, reportedly even more frequently than the eagle. Political post cards from the 1904, 1908 and 1912 campaigns often used the Teddy Bear as a symbol for Roosevelt.

Clifford K. Berryman, political cartoonist for the "Washington Post" and later for the "Washington Star," copyrighted, in 1907, two illustrations that were later used on post cards.

These cards featured the famous bear cub with Roosevelt as a "rough rider" and another with Roosevelt dressed in his long presidential coat with the Washington D.C. landscape in the background of each.

In 1904, Roosevelt declared he was not a candidate for re-election in the 1908 campaign. A post card designed by C. Barnes, copyrighted in 1907 by T.R. Gaines of New York and published by Novelty Company of Rhode Island, expressed the fear that the Teddy Bear craze was over. The verse stated by the Teddy Bear sitting on Roosevelt's shoulder was:

> Mr. President, I feel blue,
> And I scarce know what to do.
> For I have been told to-day
> That a third term you won't stay.
> Tell me quickly it's absurd,
> This rumor that I just have heard.
> For if to run you don't agree,
> My finish I can plainly see.

The Providence Novelty Company cleverly chose a doll to express the opposing opinion:

> The Little Dolly says:
> Dear Mr. President be firm,
> And don't accept a third term,
> Teddy Bears for years, you know
> Have caused us dolls lots of woe,
> Please don't run 'twill end this fad
> And make every dolly glad.
> We'll forgive the harm you've done
> If you promise not to run.

POLITICAL AND SOCIAL HISTORY 17

51
52
53
54
55
56

Two versions of this post card were published, one in full color, the other in sepia.

Another post card copyrighted 1907 by T.R. Gaines and signed by illustrator C. Barnes, features dolls carrying militant signs that read, "We have had enough of Teddy Bears," and "Teddy Roosevelt for a third term, NEVER!" This bipartisan attitude of the Gaines' publishing company was typical of that era. For example, many publishers issued both pro and anti-suffrage post cards. The same year, the New York office of Franz Huld Publishing issued a post card featuring an Uncle Sam Teddy Bear.

True to his word, Roosevelt did not run for a third term in 1908, but he was influencial in having his Secretary of War, William H. Taft, nominated. This is reflected in a post card published by W.M. Linn and Sons of Columbus, Ohio, which features a Teddy Bear dressed in a Rough Rider outfit and carrying a big stick with the slogan "Me for Taft."

A cartoon published in the "Atlantic Constitution" said, "If 'Teddy Bear' why not 'Billy Possum'?" It depicted Taft holding a possum. The cartoon was reproduced in post card form by the Lester Book and Stationery Company of Atlanta, Georgia.

It became popular to depict Taft with the possum image. Taft was inaugurated in March of 1909 and several post cards copyrighted 1909 feature the possum (Taft) taking over for the Teddy Bear

(Roosevelt). Rudolph Brothers of Philadelphia had the possum putting "Teddy" on a train to leave Washington, while Fred Lounsbury had the Teddies taking a back seat and "Billy Possum to the Front" in a post card from series 2517. Lounsbury also indicated "Uncle Sam's New Toy" was a possum as the Teddy Bear lay discarded under the chair.

Shortly after Taft's election, Roosevelt became disillusioned with Taft's handling of the office of President. It may have started with what is referred to as the "Charlie incident." Taft was reported as saying his brother Charlie had given him the Presidency. Roosevelt responded that Charlie may have given Taft the money but he, Roosevelt, had given him the nomination. Roosevelt's disappointment in Taft was an accumulation of what Roosevelt perceived as Taft's rebutal of the press and his slow decision making which led to quick compromise in order to relieve conflict. This conflict between Taft and Roosevelt can be seen in political post cards such as the one designed by Crite and copyrighted by L. Gulick in 1909. The image has the possum devouring a roasted Teddy Bear.

Early in 1910 Roosevelt accepted a Smithsonian trip to Africa. When he returned M. Periolat published a post card designed by Seed showing a child exchanging his "Teddy Bear" for a "Teddy Lion."

By 1912 Roosevelt was so disappointed in the accomplishments of Taft, he threw his hat in the ring once more. The Republican convention that year, after much debate, renominated Taft. A few weeks later, Roosevelt was nominated to a New Progressive Party ticket. The post card messages included, "I won't be happy till I get my teddy back." However, with a split Republican ticket, both Taft and Roosevelt lost to Woodrow Wilson.

Besides being politically involved, Teddy Bears were also Suffragettes! Two such examples are portrayed on post cards. One is subtle in that only the cuff of an English bobby (policeman) is visable dragging off a Teddy who wears the militant suffrage colors of green, white and violet over her wounded eye. The other depicts a policeman arresting "Christabear" which is a direct reference to Christabel Pankhurst, a leading suffragette in England.

Because of the political and social history interest in this type of teddy bear collectible, (and the fact that they were scarce to begin with) these items are more expensive than most teddy bear post cards.

Advertising

Today, in the advertising media, a Teddy Bear is used as a symbol of security and comfort, but even at the turn-of-the century the appeal of bears was evident.

With advertisers recognizing the increasing popularity of the Teddy Bear, bears appeared often on advertising premiums. However, some of the most difficult Teddy Bear post cards to find are those relating to advertising.

The rarest of the Teddy Bear advertising post cards are those promoting the sale of Steiff bears.

One such post card published by the Steiff company, used a commercially produced photographic style post card showing a menagerie of Steiff stuffed animals boarding an arc.

The promotional information tells us that Steiff took the Grand Prize at the 1904 Saint Louis Exposition and the 1910 Brussel's Exposition. The famous Steiff trademark, "Knoff in Ohr" (button in the ear) was displayed on the front of the card. The one known example was post ally used in 1915.

Two other post cards advertising Steiff bears were published for the use of the Morgan Importing Company, 136 Fifth Avenue, New York, New York. The examples shown were postally used in 1907.

62

63

64

20 ADVERTISING

Cracker Jack designed a set of sixteen post cards, featuring the "**Cracker Jack Bears.**" Published in 1907, by B.E. Moreland, this is one of the most sought after post card advertising sets. They originally were sent free upon the receipt of ten side panels from boxes of Cracker Jack or ten cents and one side panel, from the manufacturer of Rueckheim Brothers and Eckstein of Chicago, Illinois. The cards are slightly smaller than the standard post card size and are flat-printed in color.

ADVERTISING **21**

81

82

83

84

85

Teddy Bear Bread, made by the New England Bakery of Pawtucket, Rhode Island, came in two size loaves priced at five and ten cents each. The advertising post cards for this product are scarce. The scarcity of the cards was created by the fact that a Teddy Bear stick pin was given away as a premium upon turning in a set of cards. The post cards, of course, were immediately destroyed by the merchant. This four card set tells a story of a Teddy Bear finding a loaf of bread and selling it. The cards were designed by W.W. Denslow.

86
87
88
89
90
91

Another highly desirable advertising post card set was a 1907 group of six cards published by Buchan's Soap. For the return of a wrapper of 363 soap by Buchan, the series of six post cards were sent to the consumer.

While many other cards do exist featuring the Teddy Bear as an advertising agent, such as the Listerate Pepsin Gum series which featured Teddies with Pepsin gum trademarks on their chests, cards for Culver Cub Shoes, Ovaltine, even an ad for Teddy Bear rings, keep in mind to be a true advertising post card the card should have been designed to sell a specific product.

However, many Teddy Bear post cards have been used to imprint store advertising messages, such as book store overprints and wallpaper ads on the Roosevelt Bear series. The Busy Bear post cards were often used to imprint messages (see p.38).

24 ADVERTISING

92

93

94

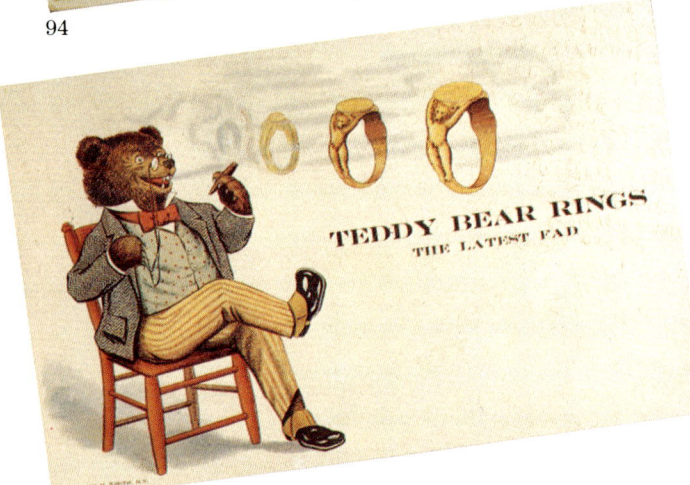
95

96

97

Artist Signed Post Cards

Today, it is difficult to establish who the artist is on commercially produced graphics; sometimes it may even be the work of several talents. However, many of the post cards produced during the golden age, 1898 to 1918, were signed by the illustrators. Yet, many of these artists are known to collectors only by name as very little biographical information is available about these very talented people. Collectors soon learn to recognize the artistic styles of such artists as Pillard, Thiele, Ellam and Hildebrand.

Many of these graphic design people worked for several publishers, doing post cards, book illustrations, magazine covers and valentines. Because nearly three million post cards were being postally processed in the United States every day during this time, it is understandable that not all post card artists could rise to such prominence as to be listed in "Who's Who in Art". Many worked for only short periods of time. Most of the commercial artists were women and their names changed with marriages. For example, Grace Gebbie signed her work as G.G. Weiderseim and G.G. Drayton, while Rose O'Neill used Latham and Wilson as she married and remarried. All these problems were compounded by the destruction of publisher's records when Europe was bombed during two World Wars.

What is important to know is that items that can be correctly identified or are signed by the artist have more value, in most cases, as the same type of material unsigned.

Atwell

Mable Lucie Atwell was an English post card artist born on June 4, 1879. Working primarily for three English post card firms; Bamforth, Tuck and Valentine Publishing. Atwell had a career of nearly 70 years producing post card images of chubby-cheeked little children. Her first works were sold at the age of 16 and she continued working until her death on November 13, 1964 in Cornwall, England, at the age of 85.

She also designed posters and children's books as did her husband Harold C. Earnshaw. Atwell had a daughter and two sons.

Brundage

Born June 28, 1854, in Newark, New Jersey, Francis Brundage was well established as a children's book illustrator by the turn-of-the-century. Her father, Rembrandt Lockwood, was an architect, wood engraver and painter. He abandoned Francis when she was in her late teens and she was forced to support herself through drawing and painting. She began by illustrating the books of Louisa May Alcott and the plays of William Shakespeare. Later, she wrote and illustrated her own books for children.

In 1886, she married William Tyson Brundage, a painter of marine life. They lived in Washington, D.C. and in New York City, where she was hired by the New York office of Raphael Tuck to illustrate children's books. Brundage made several trips to England while employed by Tuck, and began to design post cards for them around 1900.

In 1910, Brundage contracted to design post cards for Samuel Gabriel in New York City. Brundage's work also appears on valentines. She died in 1937 at the age of eighty-three.

100   101   102

Clapsaddle

In the history of American post cards, illustrator Ellen Hattie Clappsaddle was the most prolific with over two thousand signed post card illustrations and many unsigned designs to her credit.

Born January 8, 1865, in South Columbia, New York, she was an only child. In New York, she contracted to work for the International Art Company. Many of her designs were registered with the copyright office by International Art Company and Samuel Garre, the owner of the firm, during 1907-1912. The Wolf Brothers had a vested interest in the International Art Company at that time. Later, they established their own publishing house of Wolf Brothers in which Clappsaddle invested her life savings. She designed post cards for the new firm, many of which are not signed. With the start of World War I, the decline of the post card craze, and the severe shortage of paper, Clapsaddle lost her entire investment.

Her work can also be found on porcelain, calendars, die-cut scraps, posters, greeting cards and valentines. Clapsaddle died in the Peabody Home in New York City on January 7, 1934, one day before her 69th birthday.

103   104   105   106

ARTIST SIGNED POST CARDS

Colombo

Drayton
(see page 103 for biographical sketch)

107

Ebner

Ellam
W.H. Ellam was an English artist who created many post card designs featuring Teddy Bears. He worked for both English and German publishers. See p.39-41 in sets.

109   110

Fisher
Harrison Fisher was born in Brooklyn, New York, on July 27, 1875, but moved to California as a child. His father, Hugo A. Fisher was an artist and Harrison's talent was recognized at an early age. He began his career in commercial art doing staff illustrations and sketches of accidents for the "San Francisco Call" and later the "San Francisco Examiner." He was transferred to New York where he sold sketches of women to "Puck" and illustrated many other contemporary magazines including "Scribner's," "Cosmopolitan," "Life," "McClures," as well as nearly 100 illustrations and covers for "Saturday Evening Post." Fisher is recognized as one of America's foremost illustrators and the "King of Magazine" illustration.

The Fisher designs for which Charles Scribner's Sons held the copyright were published on post cards by Reinthal and Newman of New York. Fisher died in New York January 19, 1934.

111   112

Gassaway

Katherine Gassaway designed cards for several publishers including Rotograph, National Art, Tuck and Ullman during the period 1906-1909. Her children are distinctly drawn and easily recognized as her work.

113

114

115

116

Gutmann

This image was issued as an 18 by 24 inch print by "Ladies Home Journal" in 1907 for $1.00 in black and white and $1.50 for hand coloring.

Nystrom

Jenny Nystrom was born in Kalmar, Sweden. She designed post cards, newspaper and magazine illustrations and over 250 different book covers and produced water color and oil paintings.

Hays

An accomplished artist and author, Margaret Hays was also the sister of Grace Gebbie Drayton-Weiderseim.

117

118

ARTIST SIGNED POST CARDS **29**

119
120
121
122
123
124
125

Agnes Richardson
(see page 89 for biographical sketch)

Rockwell

An outstanding American illustrator, Norman Rockwell's work is well known to collectors.

The card shown here was produced as a salesmen's calling card for the Upjohn Company, Kalamazoo, Michigan and its regional offices.

Theile

Arthur Theile, a German artist was born in 1841 and died at the age of 65.

126

127
128
129

130

Twelvetrees

Charles Twelvetrees was an American illustrator and designer. Best known to doll collectors for his 1926 creation of the "HEbee-SHEbee" doll for Horsman Doll Company, Twelvetrees was also a successful magazine illustrator with covers done for "Pictorial Review" on a regular basis.

Twelvetrees was a prolific post card artist, specializing in comical post cards featuring round-faced children. He designed cards for Edward Gross Publishing and the National Art Company.

In 1906 he produced a six card set for National Art Company featuring Teddy Bears. The cards numbered (206-211) are as follows: "Little Bear Behind," "Stung," (see sheet music section), "The Bear on the Dark Stairway," "How can you bear this weather?," "A Bear Impression," and "The Seashore Bear."

Twelvetees spent much of his life in New York City, and died there April 7, 1948.

131

132

ARTIST SIGNED POST CARDS **31**

133

Wain

Born in 1860, in England, Louis Wain's name became a household word by the turn of the century. He depicted the social history of his time with drawings of cats behaving as young grown-ups rather than children. His mind failed and he was admitted in poverty to a mental institution. When discovered, a group of influential people established a fund to cover his care in a private facility. He died in 1939.

Wall 134

Bernhardt Wall was born in Buffalo, New York, December 30, 1872. At the age of 22, his ability was such that he opened his own studio to train artists, however his teaching ended when he enlisted in the army during the Spanish-American War. After the War he took a position with the Ullman Manufacturing Company designing prints to help sell their picture frames. Later, Ullman entered the post card publishing business. Wall then became well known for his Sunbonnet girls with their bright red dresses and white bonnets. Nearly as popular was his Busy Bear series which he designed for Ullman. (See page 40 in Sets Chapter.)

Wall designed post cards for nearly fifteen different post card companies including Barton and Spooner, International Art, Illustrated Post Card Company and the Gibson Art Company.

Wall became a professional etcher in 1913. His works are found today in many museums. He died February 9, 1956, at the age of eighty-three, in Los Angeles, California.

135

136

Wood

English artist Lawson Wood lived from 1878 to 1957. Wood worked for Valentine Post Card Company of Great Britian. He designed many advertising calendars, blotter and magazine covers. He is best remembered for his classic "Collier's" covers featuring monkeys.

137

138 139 140 141 142 143

John Winsch, Publisher

John O. Winsch, of Stapleton, New York, first issued his copyrighted line of post cards in 1910. From his office at 147 5th Avenue, New York City, New York, he sold large quantities of his superior greetings at two for five cents until he ceased publication in 1915.

Like many post cards of that era, the Winsch line was actually printed in Germany. Winsch copyrighted nearly 3,000 designs during that five year period, with less than 300 being done in 1915.

Winsch hired many artists from both the United States and Europe, but according to copyright records, all Winsch's Santas were done by German artists.

The above cards range from 1910 to 1913 in copyright dates. The cards are highly embossed and represent some of the best Winsch Teddy Bear images.

Post Card Sets

Just as the Teddy Bear was becoming a national obsession, post cards were in their golden era. The publishers took advantage of every opportunity to create post cards of new and exciting designs. It is little wonder that so many cards appeared featuring the Teddy Bear.

During the post card craze, 1898 to 1918, contests were devised by major post card publishers, such as Raphael Tuck of England, with large cash prizes given for albums containing the most "postally" used cards printed by their company. This created an even greater interest in collecting and exchanging post cards with friends.

It was at this time that most parlors contained three major books: the family bible, a photograph album and the post card album.

However, even without the collecting aspect of early post cards, they were in great demand as a primary means of communication. Telephones were not common, and mail service was frequent, often two or three times daily. But it must be remembered that even though this service was provided for one or two cents, the average person did not have friends who lived much beyond ten miles away or the distance of a good buggy ride.

While post cards were initially issued as singles, it became a marketing device to issue post cards in groups or sets of 4, 6, 8 or more cards.

There is not a specific number of post cards in a set, however, there are some general rules. Italian publishers preferred sets of four; Raphael Tuck and most European publishers issued sets of six or multiples of six. Many complete sets are featured here to help researching collectors.

Some post card sets are not original post card designs but reprinted designs from books. One such set was published in 1907 by Thayer Publishing Company of Denver, Colorado. Designed by Fred L. Cavally, Jr. the set was reproduced from the illustrations of *Mother Goose's Teddy Bears* published by Bobbs Merrill Company.

POST CARD SETS

POST CARD SETS **35**

Molly on the Garden Wall
160

Molly's Charge
161

Teddy's Nurse
162

Teddy's Capture
163

If Teddy were a Man
164

Rambles of Molly and Teddy
165

Magnus Greiner worked for International Art where she designed series 791. The set is so popular with post card collectors that the set and each card within the set has been given titles, even though no titles appear on the cards. The set has been called **The Adventures Of Molly and Teddy.**

The set comes embossed and flat with and without Christmas greetings. Several dozen other International Art post cards have the Greiner signature, but these are the only bears.

POST CARD SETS

166
167
168
169
170
171

This page:

    Fritz Hildebrand designed these charming cards for publisher Raphael Tuck & Sons. They were produced as "**Teddy Bär**," No. 549 for the German market and "**Teddy Bear, Series 1**" (No. 9792) for the English market.

Card titles (Opposite page)

"TUCK LITTLE BEARS"

Left hand cards — top to bottom:
"ONE IN THE EYE"
THE JOLLY ANGLERS
"MISSED AGAIN"
THE CAKE WALK
TOBOGGANING IN THE SNOW
KEPT AT SCHOOL

Right hand cards:
"YOUR GOOD HEALTH"
"THE ICE BEARS BEAUTIFULLY"
A VERY FUNNY SONG
A MORNING DIP
BREAKING THE RECORD
OH, WHAT A SHOCK!

POST CARD SETS 37

POST CARD SETS

184

185   186   187

These twelve post cards were published by J.I. Austin based on illustrations from the book *"The Busy Bears,"* written by George W. Gunn. Series 427-432 were printed several times resulting in different images appearing with the same caption. For example, Saturday was illustrated with both baking and mending. Series 433-438 feature school activities. While some of the book's 14 illustrations, including front and back cover, were in black and white, all post cards are in color. (The cards are pictured in the same order as they appear in the book.)

POST CARD SETS **39**

40 POST CARD SETS

198 — TUESDAY — This Little Bear Irons Clothes.
197 — MONDAY — This Little Bear Washes Clothes.
199 — WEDNESDAY — This Little Bear Mends Clothes.
200 — THURSDAY — This Little Bear Bakes Pies.
201 — FRIDAY — This Little Bear Cleans House.
202 — SATURDAY — This Little Bear Goes to Market.
203 — SUNDAY — This Little Bear Goes to Church.

Ullman published the "**Days of the Week Bears**" series number 79, drawn by Bernhardt Wall and referred to by the publisher as the "**Busy Bears.**"

POST CARD SETS **41**

204 205 206 207 208 209

These playful teddy bears were created by artist W.H. Ellam and were published by Faulkner (Series 902) and Druck Verlag von B. Dondorf (Series 347).

Page 42:
Post cards by W.H. Ellam by a variety of publishers

Page 43:
Raphael Tuck and Sons, art publishers to their majesties the King and Queen, Oilette series #9793 **"Teddy Bears at the Seaside"** (top six cards) **"Bears at Play"** by Tuck (bottom four cards).

42 POST CARD SETS

210

211

212

213

214

215

216

217

218

Cards by W.H. Ellam

POST CARD SETS 43

Cards by W.H. Ellam

44 POST CARD SETS

229

230

231

232

233

POST CARD SETS 45

234

235

236

The rivalry between the doll and the Teddy Bear for the affection of children and a larger share of the retail market is illustrated by these two sets, published by T.P. & Company of New York City.
(Note: each set contains six cards.)

237

238

239

240

241

242

243

244

This page:

In 1907, William S. Heal published a set of post cards with bears engaging in weekday activities. Monday's bear washed clothes...Sunday's bear went to church. This set was published both on paper and on leather.

Page 47:

J. Ottmann Lithographing Company published this ten card set in 1907 in New York City. They are lithographed in nine colors and embossed on bristol board.

POST CARD SETS 47

48 POST CARD SETS

These artist's creations became known as "**Rose Clark Bears.**" Published in 1907 by Rotograph Company of New York City, and designed by Rose Clark, the series is numbered 307-318.

POST CARD SETS **49**

97-1 267
97-2 268
97-3 269
97-4 270
97-5 271
97-6 272

Another popular but confusing set is actually five series of six different images, creating 30 different post cards. Published by Tower Manufacturing and Novelty Company of New York, "Playthings" magazine attributed them to Stephen T. Buckhan, a buyer and manager of the post card department at Tower.

The bears are dressed in stripes and polka dot outfits and each card is numbered as series 97 with an individual card number to follow. The six cards are 97-1 through 97-6. Each number has five different variations of the same design but each has a unique message.

The complete set consists of:

97-1 I would Like to be your Little Bear	97-2 It's a Skin Game	97-3 Greetings from…	97-4 "Hurrah" for the American Eagle, That beautiful Bird so hale; Whom nobody can inveigle, Or put Salt on his lovely tail.	97-5 Good Morning
97-1 This is the strenuous Life	97-2 Our cousins in their mountain lair, Are not in style they're just plain bear.	97-4 Here's to the Stars and Stripes, The Land of our Birth, A Pretty Girl -The best Things-on-Earth	97-4 Greetings from…	97-5 Smoke Up
97-1 But we are civilized quite, Therefore they dress us "out of sight"	97-2 Greetings from…	97-4 Did you ever wear Stripes?	97-5 Heads or tails	97-5 Greetings from…
97-1 I am Waiting For You	97-3 The ladies love us every day, And winning things they to us say.	97-4 Our birth you know was very grand, We saw the light in Freedom's Land.	97-5 We wear pajamas and have perfume too, We are two dandies from the Polar Zoo.	97-6 There is Trouble Bruin.
97-1 Greetings From…	97-3 You Don't Say			97-6 Keep it Quiet
97-2 "Beary" Well, Thank You.	97-3 Don't Say a Word			97-6 Let Us Reform
97-2 Lost, Strayed, Or Stolen	97-3 Won't you Join us?			97-6 The children too must have a pet - If you are not a bear you may be one yet.
				97-6 Greetings from…

POST CARD SETS

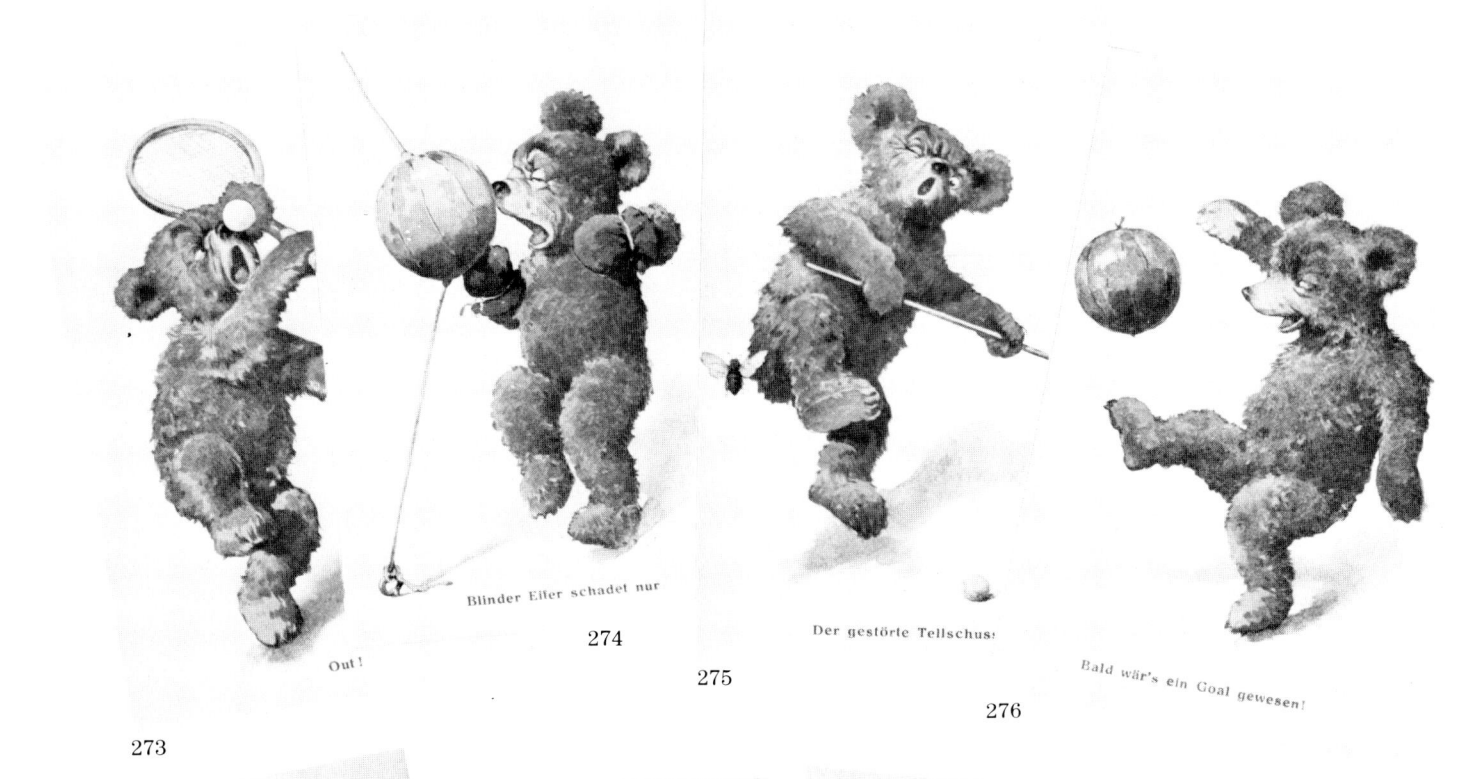

273 274 275 276

277 278 279 280

This page:

Published in Austria, BKWI's Series 120 (top four cards) depicts action sports, while Series 3385 (bottom four cards) shows Teddy Bears engaging in winter recreation.

Page 51:

BKWI's series 79 (four cards on left shows Teddy Bears in a circus atmosphere, while series 67 (four cards on right) has the young bears experiencing the joys of formal education.

Page 52:

BKWI's Series 62 (top four cards) depicts Teddy Bears learning the finer "points" of cactus raising. Series 80 (four center cards) combines music and a parade of gift-bearing Teddy Bears and Series 81 (bottom four cards) shows the bears exhibiting their musical abilities.

POST CARD SETS 51

281 Der tüchtige Jongleur

282 Kurz ist der Wahn und lang ist die Reu

283 Uraufführung

284 Stimmt an das Lied vom Teddybär

285 Generalprobe

286 Wer nicht hören will, muß fühlen

287 Theaterskandal

288 Und bist du nicht willig, so brauch ich Gewalt

52 POST CARD SETS

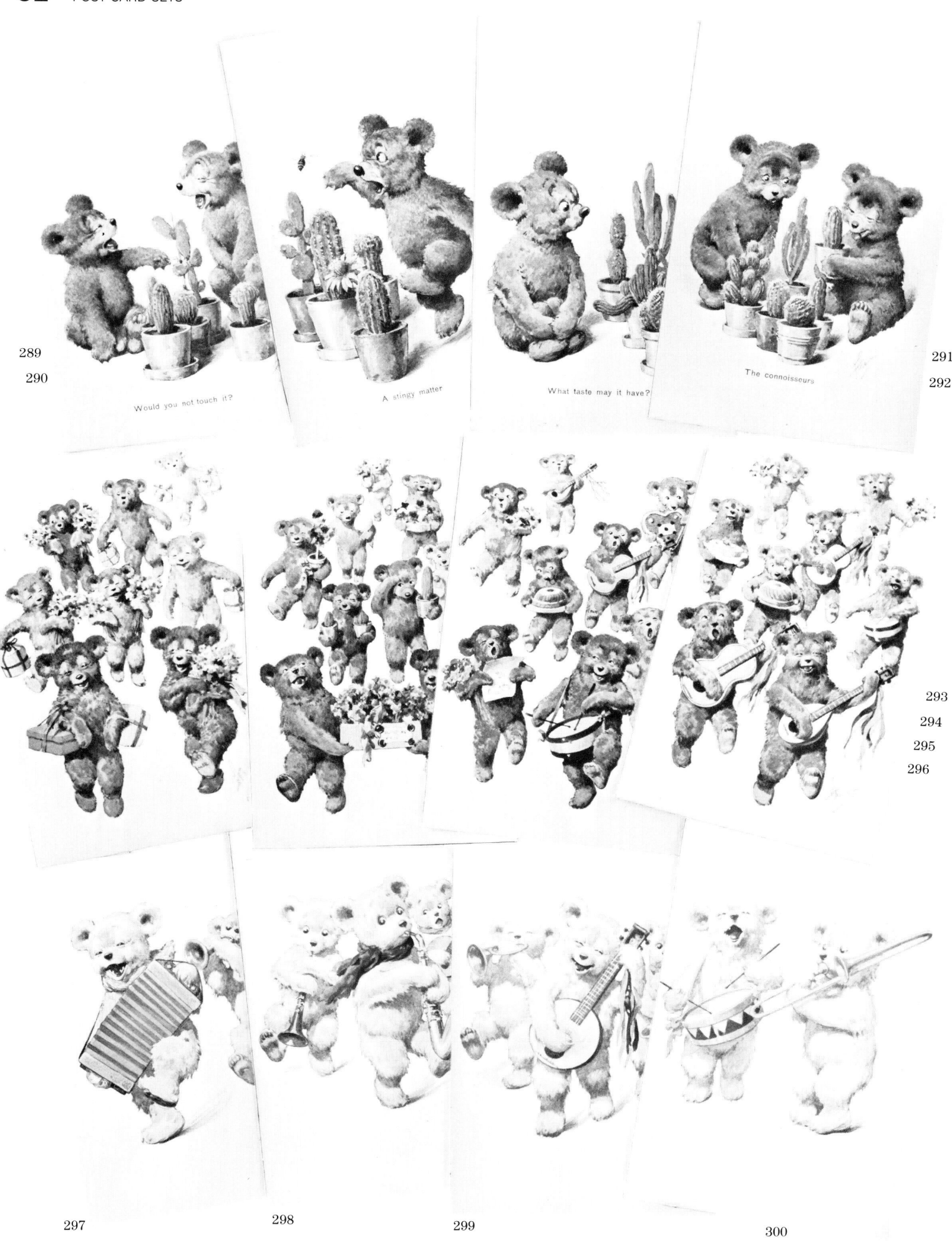

289
290

Would you not touch it?

A stingy matter

What taste may it have?

The connoisseurs

291
292

293
294
295
296

297   298   299   300

POST CARD SETS 53

The H.G. Zim Company published the "**Crane Bears**" series.

54 POST CARD SETS

308
309
310
311
312
313
314

In 1907, D. Hillson issued the 600 series of "**Bears in Green**" following the days of the week theme. The Hillson bears washed on Monday, ironed on Tuesday, mended on Wednesday, baked on Thursday, cleaned on Friday, shopped on Saturday and went to church on Sunday. This set was printed on linen textured paper.

(Note: these post cards were also published in red.)

POST CARD SETS **55**

315

316

317

318

319

This page:

Don McGill's humor highlights the Kismet Series (Nos. 346, 347, 348, 349 & 350), which were published in London.

Page 56:

Pillard produced series 730 (top six cards) and series 759 (bottom three cards) for publisher Langsdorff and Company, London, England.

56 POST CARD SETS

The Spirit of the Teddy Bear

As the popularity of the Teddy Bear increased, more and more post card publishers included the Teddy image in their designs.

While these cards are not always done by major post card artists, or were even published in sets, they are interesting because they show a certain spirit of the Teddy Bear.

The bears dressed up in military uniforms, night caps, and bathing suits. They cuddled old maids as well as children. They were small bundles being stuffed into Santa's sack, and were nursery toys bigger than their owners.

Teddy Bears are apt to appear on any type of post card.

329

330

331

332

58 SPIRIT OF THE TEDDY BEAR

333

Here's to the ladies
God bless 'em
We can't do anything
with 'em, -
And we can't do any-
thing - without 'em.

334

RALLY DAY for the CRADLE-ROLL

"The little one shall become a thousand
and the small one a strong nation."
Isa 60:22

RALLY DAY NEXT SUNDAY
Come Babies dear, we all must go.
For we are members, and you know
If one of us should stay away,
We would be missed on RALLY DAY

335

Bonne Année

336

337

Left luggage!

338

339

SPIRIT OF THE TEDDY BEAR **59**

347
348
349
350
351

SPIRIT OF THE TEDDY BEAR **61**

352

353

354

355

356

357

358

359

360

361

SPIRIT OF THE TEDDY BEAR **63**

362

"Bosom Friends."
363

364

THE NEW LOVE.
365

366

SPIRIT OF THE TEDDY BEAR **65**

66 SPIRIT OF THE TEDDY BEAR

385

386   387   388

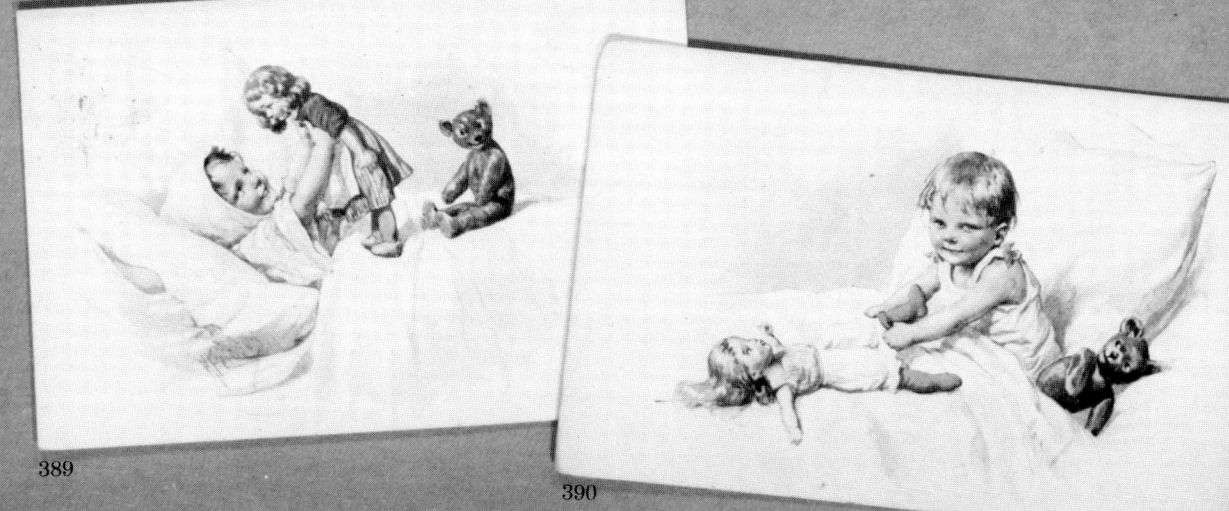
389   390

SPIRIT OF THE TEDDY BEAR **67**

391 Le plus heureux des trois.
392
393
394 La Fille à l'Ours.
395 Les favoris de Baby.
396 Pour ce baiser, le monde entier.

68 SPIRIT OF THE TEDDY BEAR

SPIRIT OF THE TEDDY BEAR **69**

403

404

405

406

407

408

Veselé vánoce!

TOM TUCKER AND THE TEDDYBEARS
ARE SINGING FOR THEIR SUPPER
WHAT SHALL WE GIVE THEM
PLUM CAKE OR BREAD AND BUTTER

Many happy returns of the Day

409

Spiel mit!

Atelier Ostermann-Wien

70 SPIRIT OF THE TEDDY BEAR

410
411
412
413
414
415
416
417
418

425

426

427

428

429

430

Novelty Post Cards

The public demand for more unusual post card designs led to increased competition between publishers. During the golden age of post cards (1898-1918), publishers became more and more creative with their products.

A direct result of this fevered pitch to increase sales was the creation of novelty post cards. Publishers added scraps of silk, felt, fur and other fabrics to give the post cards added interest. They cut the cards into die-cut shapes, (see back cover) added metal ornaments, glass eyes to dolls and bears, and even printed designs on sheepskin which had been tanned by a vegetable process. These leather cards were produced in great quantities. A major publisher of leather post cards was William S. Heal. The familiar trademark of a letter "H" with a "w" above the cross bar and an "s" below will identify his work.

A "Teddy Bear Days of the Week" set appeared on leather and several other Teddy Bear motifs. One leather card depicted Teddy Roosevelt in the shape of a bathtub, which was titled Teddy Bear, a definite play on words. Other leather post cards were issued in die-cut shapes of bears. Some of these post cards were attached to luggage-type tags made of paper to be used for the address.

Several manufacturers made finger or face puppet post cards by cutting holes in appropriate places to enhance the design. One card pictured here was designed to have fingers placed in the holes to create the illusion of legs. Some novelty cards of this type have eyes and noses cut out so the card could be worn as a mask.

Raphael Tuck and V.O. Hammon produced post cards perforated as jigsaw puzzles. After a message had been written, the card was separated into pieces and mailed. The recipient had to assemble the puzzle to read the message. Other novelty post cards had actual gramaphone records attached that played birthday messages or other delightful tunes.

431

As the ever increasing demand for novelty post cards emerged, publishers became more and more creative. One result was post cards that opened to reveal an animal, insect or flower with a three-dimensional honeycomb body. One honeycomb post card features a child with a bear.

All these novelty post cards were intended to be sent through the mail. However, following a 1907 postal regulation, cards had to be enclosed in a glassine envelope or protective box. This was to protect the hands and equipment of the postal workers since novelty cards used ground glass beads, ground metal glitter and other very sharp ornamentations.

If advertisements for novelty post cards in trade papers were any indication, they were very profitable for the card manufacturers. Some of the more clever novelty post cards retailed for twenty-five cents each at a time when most post cards were one and two cents each. A collector looking through novelty post cards often find Teddies hiding behind doors, inside folded cards, or only visible when held to a strong light.

74 NOVELTY POST CARDS

Cloth
Velveteen
Fur
Velveteen Plush

432
433
434
435

Glass eyes

436 Pin cushion
437

438 Honeycomb
439 Embroidery

NOVELTY POST CARDS

440

441

Another unique post card item is the "Teddy Bear" post card tablet. Containing at least four pages, the tablet was designed to be cut apart and be postally used.

Highly sought after novelty post cards include cut-out or paper doll post cards. Because these had to survive not only the mailing process but the child's scissors, they demand high prices today.

76 NOVELTY POST CARDS

Paper items were also used to create novelty post cards. Pouches or pockets were added to the post card design to protect a long accordian-shaped paper attachment that offered additional views.

442

443

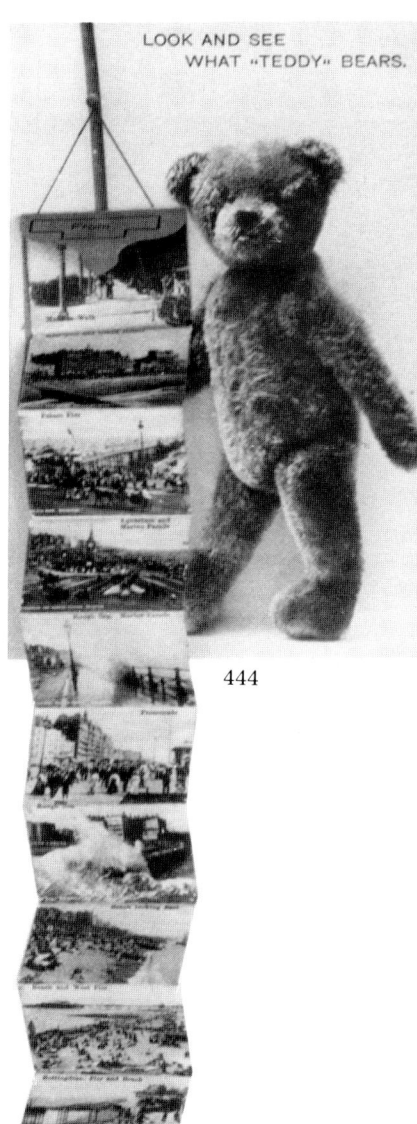

444

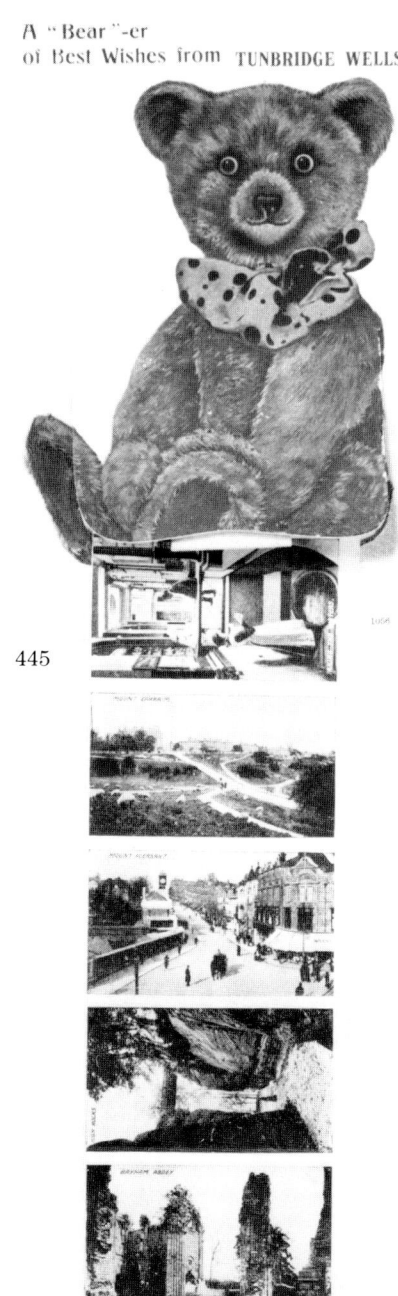

445

NOVELTY POST CARDS

There is a "Teddy" the "head" of a Nation -, But of mine he is not the slightest relation.

The novelty craze included installment sets that consisted of anywhere from three to thirty individual post cards that when properly assembled created a composite picture. The cards were intended to be sent on consecutive days until the picture was completed. One such example forms a large Teddy Bear.

The Franz Huld Publishing Company of New York produced Huld Puzzle Series Number 15 in 1907.

Starting with the foot, a different card was sent each day, ending with the head of the puzzle.

It was a clever way to entice the consumer into purchasing four cards instead of one.

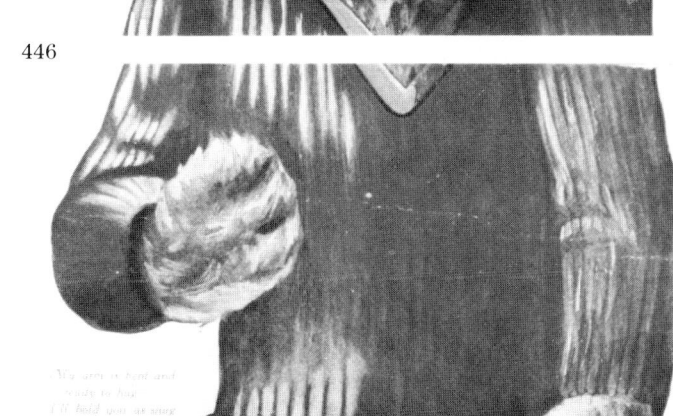

446

My arm is bent and ready to hug - I'll hold you as snug as a bug in a rug.

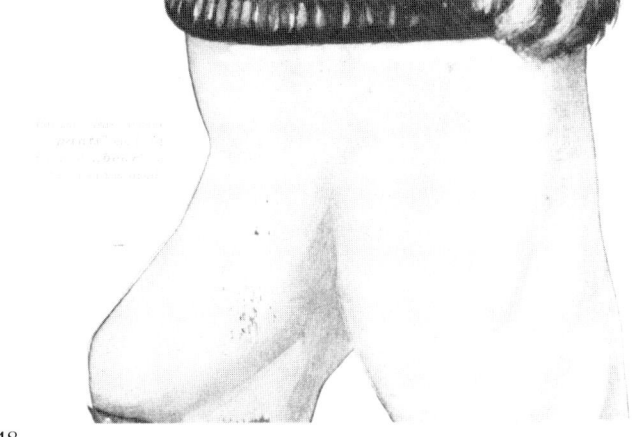

447

For you "dear" always "pants" my heart I cannot "bear" to live from you apart

448

Don't kick, because my feet I send - Though 'tis the beginning, but not the end.

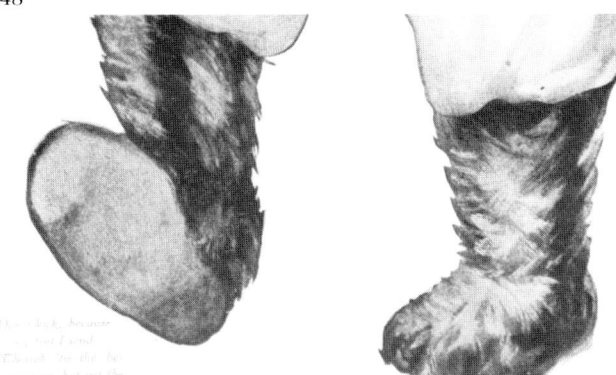

449

NOVELTY POST CARDS

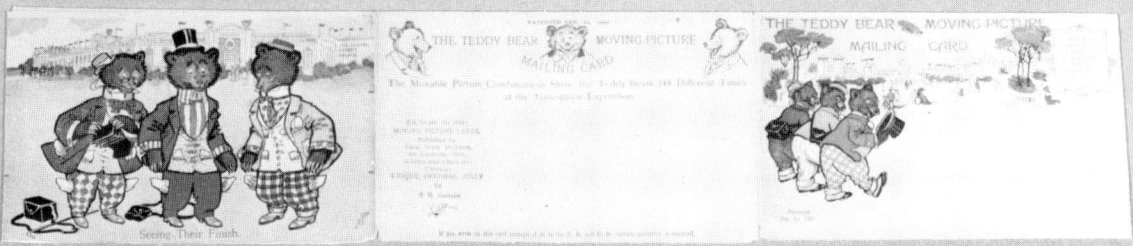

450

Prior to the 1907 Jamestown Exposition, a unique novelty post card was designed whereby the bears attending the fair could be dressed in no less than 144 outfits by merely flipping attached one-third horizontal segments of paper. This is by far the rarest of the Teddy Bear novelty post cards. Patented in 1907, the Teddy Bear Moving Picture post card was published by the Ideal Book Builders of Chicago, Illinois. The illustrations were done by R.H. Gorman.

NOVELTY POST CARDS **79**

451

452

453

During the golden age of post cards (1898-1918) Raphael Tuck publishing was the hallmark of fine quality art printing and publishing.

Raphael Tuck died in 1899 at the age of 79, but his sons Adolph, Gustave and Herman continued to produce paper dolls and toys, post cards, and greeting cards. Tuck became a public company in 1901 and in 1910, Adolph Tuck was made a baronet of the United Kingdom.

By the turn of the century, Tuck was producing nearly 40,000 different pictorial post cards.

The two post cards shown, Tuck series 3399, were also used as a part of the graphics for a Tuck Rockers Modelling book. Publishers frequently used and reused the graphic illustrations from commissioned artists. The book contained a total of fourteen rockers featuring animals and children.

454

A variety of mechanical post cards were published to amuse the consumer during the post card craze. American post card series 121 published by the Ullman Manufacturing Company of New York, number 2229, entitled "**An All Around Bear**," features a bear designed by Bernhardt Wall (note Wall signature is hidden in the grass). When the revolving disc is turned, the bear changes hats, (see biographical information on Wall under Artist signed).

455

456

One of the most interesting of these novelty type post cards used a variety of techniques to reveal formerly hidden dimensions when the post card was held up to a strong light. One such novelty is called a transparency "**Hold-to-light**" which bonded several very thin layers of paper together, resulting in an entirely different image merely by holding the card to the light. Often these consisted of Winter scenes becoming Summer scenes. Another motif featured a Bear, a Santa, or other figures at one side of the card with a large white oval on the other side. When the card was placed to the light, an image appeared in the white oval.

Another method also used several layers of paper but the top layer had die-cut holes or windows cut into the design. When held to the light, the die-cut holes resembled bright stars, candles on Christmas trees or even late night street lights. These post cards are called Die-Cut Hold-to-Lights.

Real Photo Post Cards

457

Teddy Bears have become an institution and it is easy to determine the reason for their popularity when real photographic post cards are studied. Many of these post cards are unique because itinerant photographers or family members would photograph a child with his favorite teddy and only produce a few cards from the negatives.

From these early photographic records, we know that some children had more than one bear, that Teddy was invited to tea parties and picnics and that even snowmen were formed in his image.

The Teddy Bear craze was not limited to children. It became popular for teenagers to include Teddy in class portraits and parties, even at the beach. Some of these same young people carried their Teddies to college and war.

Perhaps these young adults clinged to their bears to remind themselves of when life was simple. It is plain to see, the Teddy Bear was a companion who listened to an owner's joys and sorrow, but most of all, always understood.

American presidents, the Queen of England and Princess Margaret, sports personalities and movie stars have enjoyed and perserved their childhood Teddies. When England had a Celebriteddy Exhibition, hundreds of famous people sent their bears to participate. Today, the fascination of Teddy Bears is still a part of the adult world. Many bears are purchased by adults for adults, some are even made of mink!

82 REAL PHOTO POST CARDS

458

459

460

REAL PHOTO POST CARDS **83**

461

462

463

464

465

466

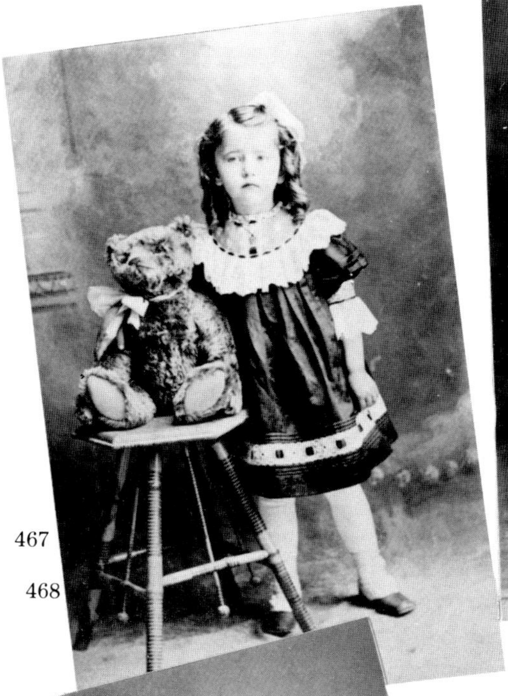

84 REAL PHOTO POST CARDS

467
468 
469 
470 
471 
472 
473 
474 
475

REAL PHOTO POST CARDS **85**

476
477 DORRIT WEIXLER
SHIRLEY TEMPLE   FOX FILM
478
479
480 ALICE HECHY
H.R.H. The DUCHESS of YORK
481
482 ANNA HELD
483
484 MISS EVA STUART

485
486
487
488
489
490
491
492

REAL PHOTO POST CARDS **87**

493
494
495
496
497
498
499
500
501

88 REAL PHOTO POST CARDS

502
503
504
505
506
507
508
509

Paper Dolls

510

Little Playmates
*Boxed Paper Dolls
By Agnes Richardson*

Raphael Tuck, a publisher to the King and Queen of England, produced a boxed set number 395 of Bonnie, Bertie and Merry Madge designed by Agnes Richardson, (1885-1951).

Richardson's lifetime home was in Wimbledon, England. The youngest of eight children, she entered many artistic competitions as a child. In 1902, Girls Realm gave her an award for a drawing of Simple Simon. Upon graduation from the Lambert School of Art, she made the rounds of the major publishing houses with her portfolio of work.

Richardson's work was well received and her career was to span more than forty years. She was a major designer of post cards for Raphael Tuck, C.W. Faulkner, Inter-Art, Photochrom, Millar and Lang, Valentine and Birn Brothers.

For many years an Agnes Richardson Annual was published by Birn Brothers. She also illustrated children's books and paper dolls.

511

Paper dolls were well established as entertainment for children, therefore, it was natural that one of the leading publishers and distributors of paper dolls released a Teddy Bear paper doll in the early 1900's. "Plaything" for 1907 advertised the Teddy Bear Paper Doll for ten cents. By October, 1911 in "Playthings" magazine, J.L. Ottmann Lithographing Company still had a full page ad listing the Teddy Bear Paper Doll in a seven inch by twelve inch envelope. This item originally sold for only ten cents and was even used as a magazine premium. Since that time, the Teddy Bear Paper Doll has been reproduced in two other sizes.

It is still a very popular paper doll. The big brown Teddy stands ten inches tall with five costumes and hats; baseball uniform, dressing gown, automobile suit, yachting suit and walking suit. Complete with envelope this is a highly desirable Teddy Bear paper item.

Four Sleeping Dolls - 1948

Queen Holden Paper Dolls

Queen Holden worked for twenty years for Whitman Publishing Company starting in 1929. In 1930, Holden drew thirty-six books for Whitman, and was greatly responsible for the early success of Whitman in the paper doll field. Holden's "Baby Nancy" established a paper doll record in 1931 with sales of over 10,000 copies. Holden's "Glamour Dolls" of

513 *Betty and Bob - 1948*

the early 40's were later the inspiration for the "Barbie Doll" of the 50's.

Holden did the following illustrated sets: Jackie and Joan - 1933; Dionne Quintuplets - 1935; Fanny Brice, Baby Snooks - 1940; Dress Me - 1943; Sleeping Dolls - 1945; Betty and Bob and Four Sleeping Dolls - 1948.

Dress Me - 1943

Queen Holden

Sleeping Dolls - 1945

Queen Holden

Jackie and Joan - 1933

PAPER DOLLS **97**

FIVE PAPER DOLLS

YVONNE · MARIE · ANNETTE · CECILE · EMELIE

SEE BACK COVER for **QUEEN HOLDEN** LARGE SIZE "QUINTIE" DOLLS with **QUEEN HOLDEN** "EASY TO DRESS" CLOTHES

EXCLUSIVE AND AUTHORIZED PHOTOGRAPHS COPYRIGHT 1935 NEA SERVICE

519

Queen Holden *Dionne Quintuplets - 1935*

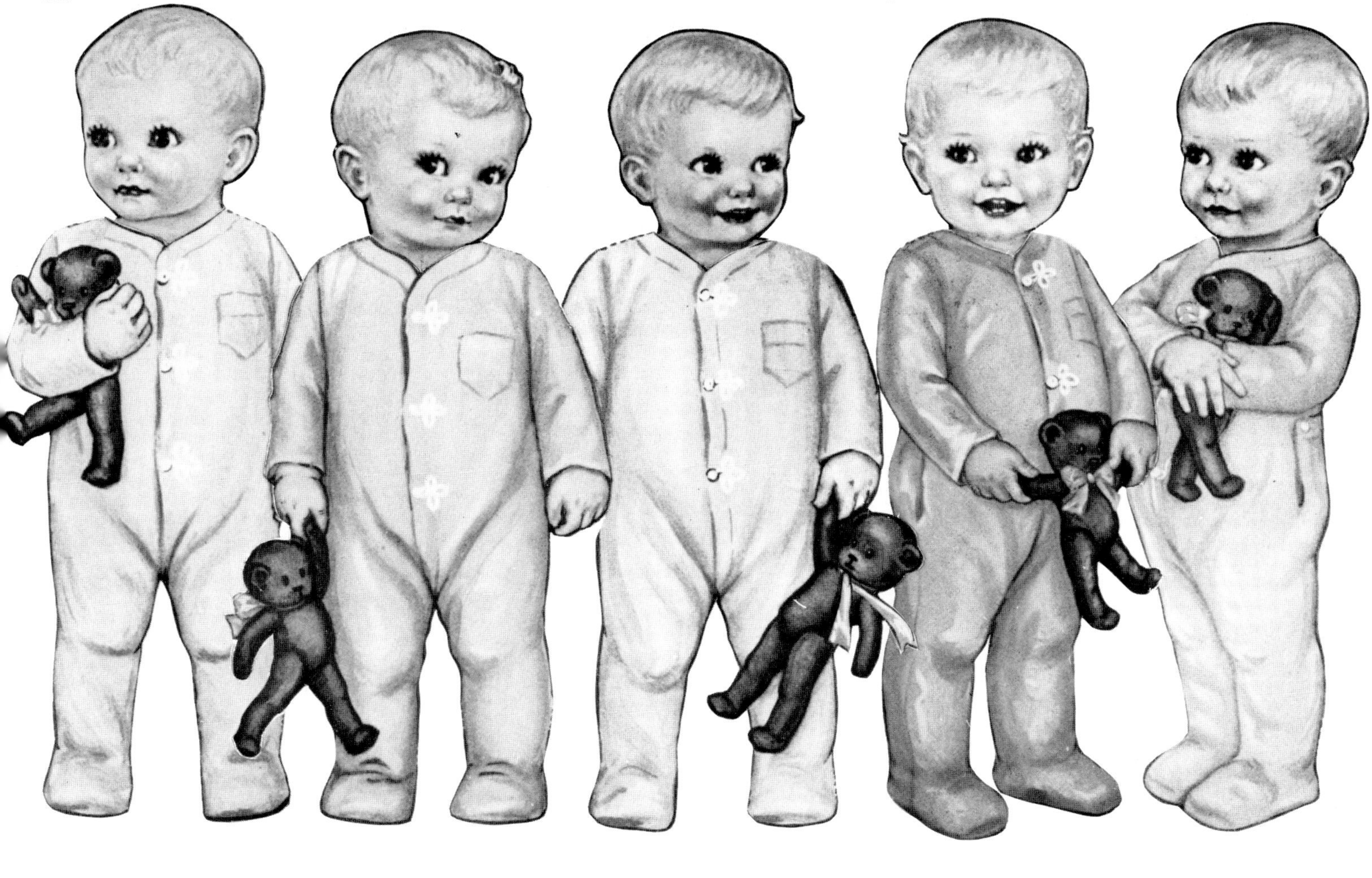

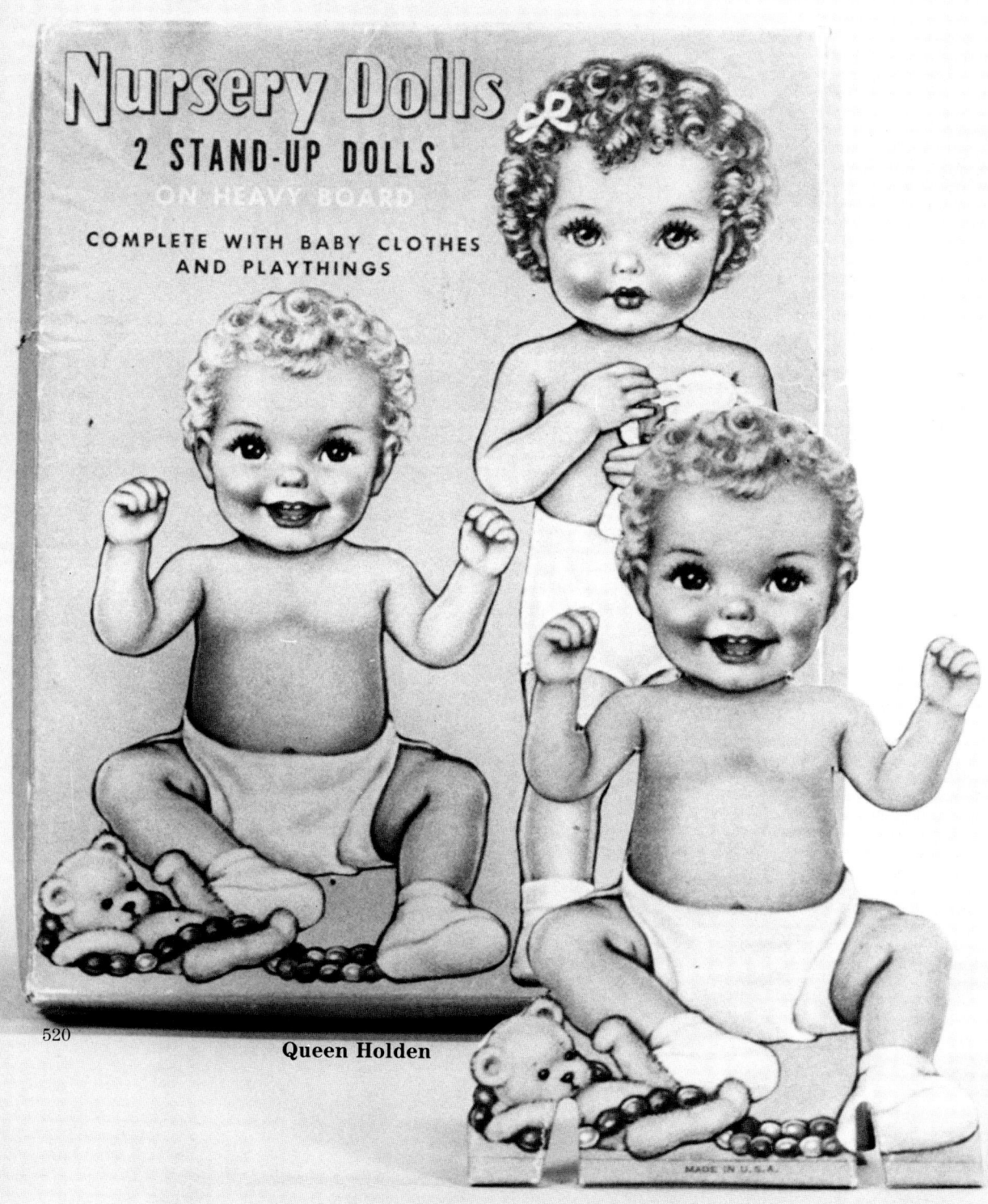

520

Queen Holden

Queen Holden
Fanny Brice, Baby Snooks - 1940

NEW
Quintuplet Dolls
5 DOLLS THAT STAND
OVER 100 PIECES TO
CUT OUT

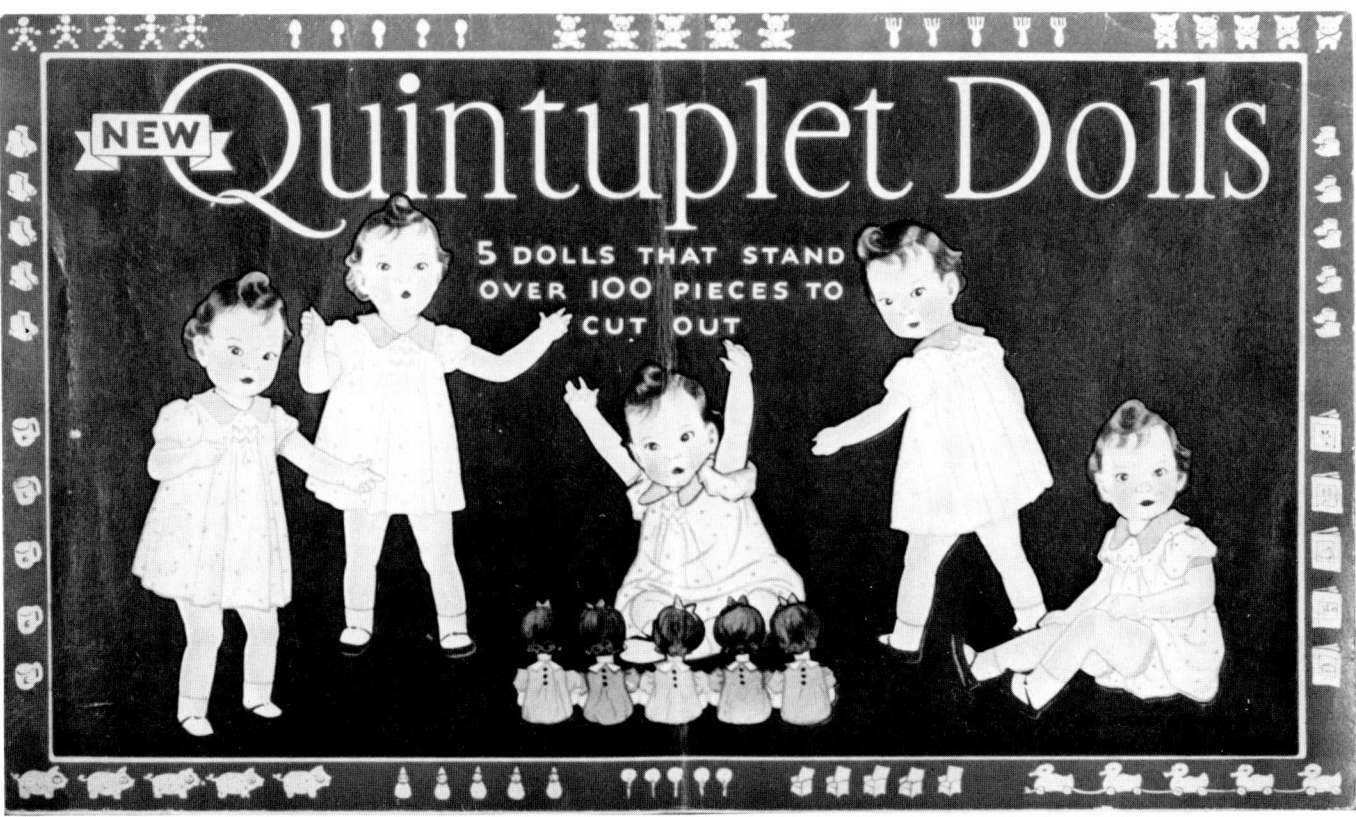

522

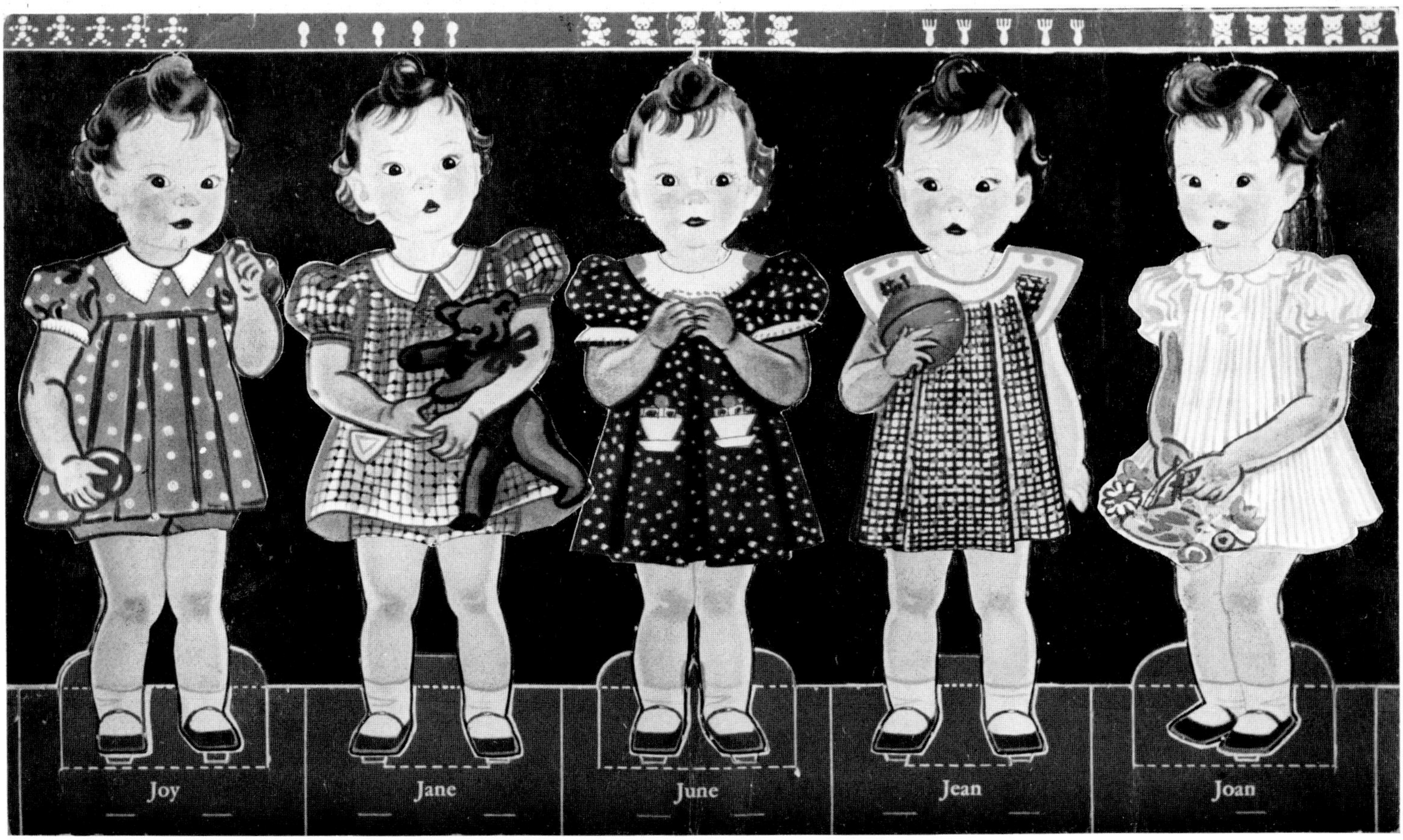
Joy
Jane
June
Jean
Joan

Shirley Temple Paper Dolls

"Shirley Temple Dolls and Dresses" was the first Shirley Temple paper doll book. It was designed by Bill and Corrine Bailey for Saalfield Publishing Company in 1934. During the next eight years Saalfield Publishing Company, who held exclusive rights of Shirley Temple paper dolls, produced ten more sets.

Saalfield Publishing Company employed Bill and Corrine Bailey from the early 1930s until the 1950s. The Bailey's produced many celebrity paper doll sets for Saalfield during their twenty years of employment. Using a special process involving an under-developed black and white photograph, an exact likeness was created by adding layers and layers of natural color to the print.

524

525

Drayton Paper Dolls

Grace (Gebbie) Wiederseim Drayton is best known for her creation of the Campbell's Soup Kids. The daughter of George Gebbie, Philadelphia's first art publisher, she was born October 14, 1877.

Grace Gebbie began her commercial art career at the age of seventeen by making place cards. The following year she sold her first magazine sketch. Grace and her sister, Margaret Gebbie Hays, worked together to produce newspaper features and books.

526

527

528

Grace Wiederseim Drayton's most collected work is her paper dolls, Dolly Dingle, and her post cards which she did for publishers such as Reinthal Newman, Schweizer, Davis and Tuck.

Drayton drew two hundred paper dolls for "Pictorial Review," seven years of weekly or daily cartoon strips, over three hundred Campbell Soup advertisements and illustrated many books. She also designed dolls, illustrated fashions and magazine covers, illustrated calendars and full-page Sunday supplements.

She was a member of the Fellowship of the Academy of Fine Arts in Philadelphia, the Author's League of America and the Society of Illustrators.

Grace married twice, first to Theodore Wiederseim, Jr., second to W. Heyward Drayton III. Both marriages ended in divorce. She died in 1936 at her home in New York City.

106 PAPER DOLLS

529
530
531
532
533
534

December 1911 Eleanor Colby

September 1913 Ella Dolbear Lee

December 1908 Sheila Young

July 1915 Sheila Young

535 536 537 538

Paper Dolls - miscellaneous sheets

Searching paper doll pages usually turns up Teddy Bears at Christmas. While many magazine illustrators such as Ella Dolbear Lee and Eleanor Colby produced occasional magazine pages, Sheila Young is well-known for her "Lettie Lane" series which appeared in the "Ladies' Home Journal." It is interesting to note that the December 1908, "Lettie Lane Paper Family" featured the monkey and Teddy Bear which belonged to Elizabeth Copeland, the niece of Sheila Young.

Sheet Music

As the Teddy Bear was introduced, Americans were enjoying the material rewards of the industrial revolution. A greater demand for sheet music was created with the increased popularity of the piano. To be more competitive, the cover pages of sheet music became graphic canvases.

There have been many songs written using the words Teddy or Teddy Bear in the title. For example, between 1907 and 1911 copyrights for over four hundred song titles were registered. Many of the titles were very similar, but the best selling and easiest title to find today is *The Teddy Bears' Picnic* by John W. Bratton, first published in 1907 by M. Witmark of New York. This was an instrumental piece. It was not until 1930 that British songwriter Jimmy Kennedy wrote the lyrics which spurred a deluge of requests for *The Teddy Bears' Picnic*.

539

540

SHEET MUSIC

541
542
543

544 *1906 post card designed by C. Twelvetrees, published by the National Art Company.*

The following is a partial listing of sheet music with the word Teddy Bear in the title or a graphic image.

A Full Hand, by Abe Losch, published by Vandersloot Music Co.
At their Noonday Rest, by Elsie Phelan
Bessie and her Little Brown Bear, by Jack Narworth and Albert Von Tilzer, published by York Music Co.
Candy, You're a Dandy
Dance of the Teddy Bear, by J.S. Fearis
Going Walking, by Elsie Phelan
Little Nemo and his Bear, by Dave Clark & Al Gumble, published by Jerome Remick Co.
March of the Teddy Bear, by J.S. Fearis
Me and My Teddy Bear, by Coots
Musical Echoes from Teddy Bear Land (a composite of 10 Teddy Bear songs by R.G. Grady)
Playing Leap-Frog, by Elsie Phelan
Playmates, by Harry J. Lincoln, Vandersloot publishing
Returning Home, by Elsie Phelan
Stung, by Theron C. Bennett, published by Victor Kremer Co.
Sunrise (awakening of the Teddy Bears) by R.G. Grady, published by Gamble Hinged Music Co.
Teddy
Teddy and Home
Teddy Bear
Teddy Bear at Home, by R.G. Grady
Teddy Bear at the Dance, by R.G. Grady
Teddy Bear Blues, by James H. Jackson, published by Sherman, Clay & Co.
Teddy Bear Coming from School, by R.G. Grady
Teddy Bear Coming from the Dance, by R.G. Grady
Teddy Bear's Dance
Teddy Bear Going to School, by R.G. Grady
Teddy Bear in an Airship, by R.G. Grady
Teddy Bear in School, by R.G. Grady
Teddy Bear in Slumberland, by R.G. Grady
Teddy Bear Pieces, by J.S. Fearis, several color variations published by McKinley Music Co.
Teddy Bear Playing Football, by R.G. Grady
Teddy Bear Rag
Teddy Bear Song
Teddy Bear's Lullaby, by Agnes Hull Prendergast
Teddy Bear Waltz, by J.S. Fearis
Teddy Come Back
Teddy Come Home
Teddy in the Jungle
Teddy's Coming Home
Teddy the Jungle Bogie-Man
Teddy Trombone March
Teddy, You're a Bear, by Ring Lardner
Teddy, We're Glad You're Here
The Big Brown Bear, by Mana-Zucca, published by G. Schirmer
The Little Teddy Bears Dress Ball, Polka-two step by Walter Pulitzer, published by M. Witmark & Sons
The Teddy Bear March, by Irene Dieterich
The Teddy Bear March and Two-Step, by Albert A. Williams
The Teddy Bear Picnic, by John Bratton
The Teddy Bear's Picnic
There's Nothing Else but Teddy, by D.J. Sullivan
Waltzing, by Elsie Phelan
Will You Be My Teddy Bear? (two different cover designs) sung by Anna Held, written by Vincent Bryan & Max Hoffman, published by Jerome Renuch & Co., cover designed after art by Archie Gun

545
546
547

548
549

OTHER PAPER TEDDIES 111

Other Paper Teddies

Die cut advertising scrap

550

551   *Food product label*

112 OTHER PAPER TEDDIES

Cigarette Card -was given away as a premium with cigarettes

552

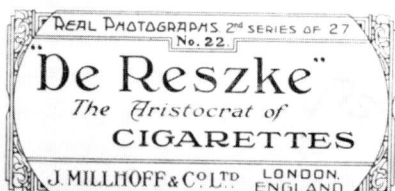

Trade card - giveaway premium

553

554   *Die cut sheet*

OTHER PAPER TEDDIES 113

556 *Miniature Grace Drayton book*

555 *Die cut calendar blank with space at top right for store name and advertisement and a printed calendar stapled to the bottom.*

557 *Die cut scrap*

Valentines

There are very few valentines using a Teddy Bear motif, even though some alluded to it with bear images. The valentine was in a decline at the time of the Teddy Bear's initial popularity. At the turn-of-the-century, about the only valentines being used to considerable extent were those printed as post cards. The new post card craze made Victorian Germany pop-up valentines a thing of the past. By World War I, the demand for valentines had greatly decreased and the paper shortage made those produced of inferior quality.

558

559 Valentine Greetings

560 Be careful how you treat me, child. This pet is woolly, strong and wild!

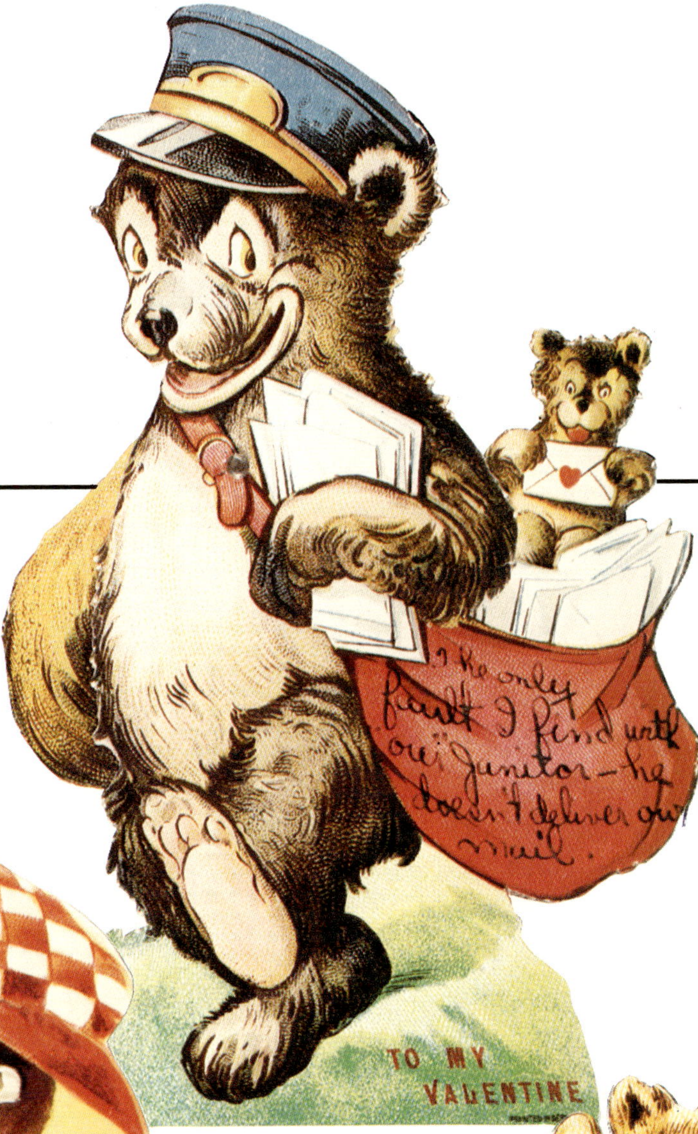
The only fault I find with our janitor—he doesn't deliver our mail.
TO MY VALENTINE

561

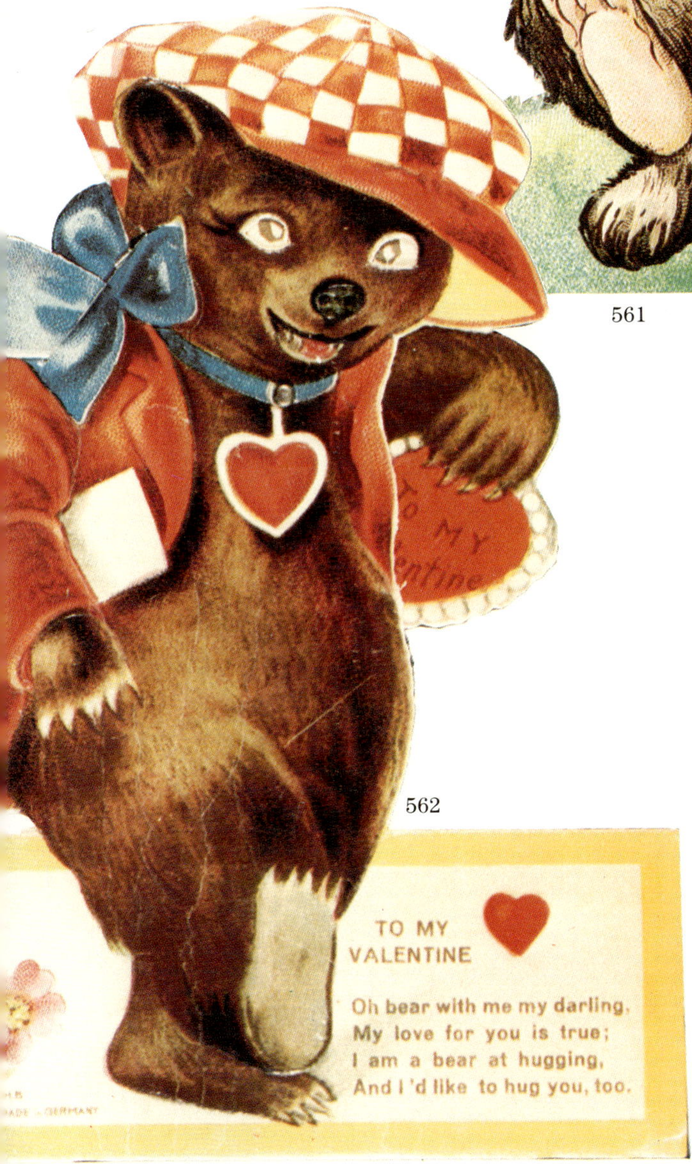
To My Valentine
TO MY VALENTINE
Oh bear with me my darling,
My love for you is true;
I am a bear at hugging,
And I'd like to hug you, too.

562

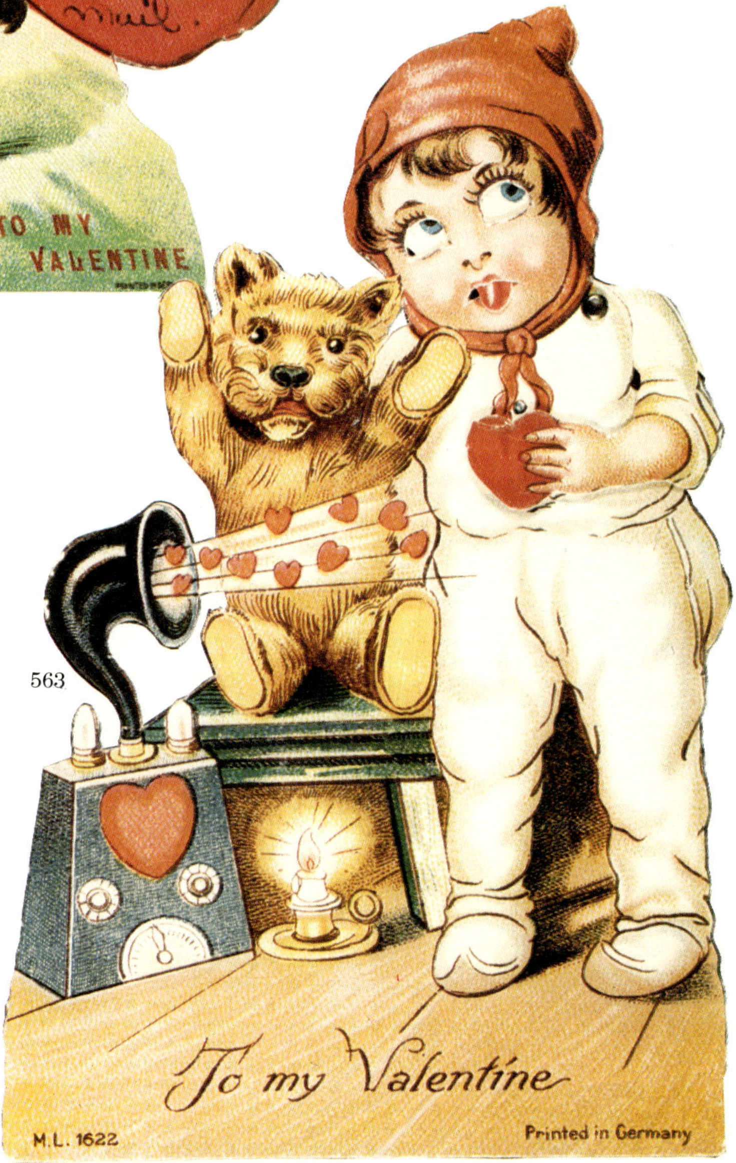
To my Valentine
M.L. 1622
Printed in Germany

563

Rockers

Raphael Tuck produced the first paper rocking toys between 1893 and 1901. However, between 1901 and 1910, Tuck upscaled their rockers, making them sturdier and more colorful.

The rockers were produced both in book form (see Toy Rockers, a Modelling book, novelty section) and boxed.

A popular boxed set, entitled "Nursery Rockers" had educational verses by Norman Gale. For example:

Off to the Party
"Now, darlings, mind you stay up there,
And don't fall off," said Mrs. Bear;
"At parties children should be neat,
And not appear with muddy feet!"

564

Raphael Tuck series number 51 is smaller in size than the "Nursery Rockers." They feature the Golliwogg and the Teddy Bear.

"Father Tuck's Toy Rocker" which contains ten different mechanical models, features a large Father Teddy in a black top hat, holding a boy teddy in one hand and a girl teddy in the other. It is titled "Joy, Joy, a well-known friend."

These popular turn-of-the-century nursery toys stand with the help of a double rocker panel, and the slightest touch will set them in motion.

565

ROCKERS 117

566

567

118 BOOKPLATES/MAGAZINE ILLUSTRATIONS

568
(6½" × 9½")

569
(6½" × 9½")

Book Plates

570
(10½" × 14½")

571
(10½" × 14½")

Magazine Illustrations
(opposite page) **Magazine Covers**

This set of Teddy Bear Playing Cards is a game that two or four can play. The object of the game is to secure all the Help Cards (15 points) and Teddy Bear Cards (20 points) and to rid yourself of the numbered cards.

Besides the set illustrated, the Teddy Bear Card Company of Erie, Pennsylvania produced a parlor game called the TEDDY BEAR CARD GAME. This pack consists of 132 cards. Three different games could be played using these cards. The wholesale price was $30.00 per 100 decks and it retailed for 50 cents per deck.

Books

While it would be impossible to list all titles of books in which Teddy Bears appear, a few key books are important to any collection.

The most sought after are the books featuring Teddy B and Teddy G, The Roosevelt Bears. The four original books published from 1906-1908 and the subsequent reprinting of these four books into ten titles in 1915 is discussed on pages 7 and 8 with illustrations.

An elusive book is *"Mother Goose's Teddy Bears,"* by Frederick L. Cavally, Jr., published by Bobbs-Merrill Company, Indianapolis, Indiana in 1907. This book has 32 color illustrations which use Teddy Bears in adapted Mother Goose rhymes. Sixteen of the color illustrations were reproduced on post cards and appear on pages 33 and 34. The cards are much easier to find than the book.

A Chicago publisher, Reilly and Britton released another popular group of eight titles in 1907. They are:

The Teddy Bears Come to Life
The Teddy Bears in a Smashup
The Teddy Bears on a Toboggan
The Teddy Bears go Fishing
The Teddy Bears at the Circus
The Teddy Bears on a Lark
The Teddy Bears at School
The Teddy Bears in Hot Water

R.D. Towne, editor of "Judge" magazine, wrote the rhymes and John Randolph Bray, a "Judge" illustrator, did the book's illustrations. The original wholesale price was 66 cents for the set of eight.

Bray was not new to Teddy Bear illustrations. He designed the first true Teddy Bear strip which appeared in "Judge." "Little Johnny and the Teddy Bears" starred a

small boy and his six little teddy bears. Their popularity was so great that the Thomas A. Edison Company produced a film called "The Teddy Bears" in which teddy bears were put through animated paces in a primitive stop-frame format. This film inspired Bray to become America's first successful animated cartoon producer.

"The Busy Bears," written by George W. Gunn and published by J.I. Austin of Chicago, had fourteen illustrations. Austin reprinted these illustrations in color on post cards which are pictured on page 38.

Other 1907 titles include, "The Wonderful Story of Teddy the Bear" written and illustrated by Sarah Noble Ives, published by McLoughlin Brother, New York; "The Teddy Bears" by Clara Andrews Williams; "The Little Toy Bearkins" by John Howard Jewett and "The Teddy Bear ABC" by Laura Rinkle Johnson, illustrated by Margaret L. Sanford, published by H.M. Caldwell Company of New York. A fantastic book which has been recently reproduced is "The Moving Picture Teddies" by R.H. Garman. One of the best known series is "Big Teddy" and "Little Teddy," written by J.C. Craddock and illustrated by Honor G. Appleton.

Teddy Bear books were produced in many countries and some of the most interesting illustrations can be found in books published abroad.

580

581

582

Featured here are two titles from a group of four books published by M.M. Nathan of Paris, France.

The texts are written in French by Constance Wickham and the superb illustrations are by A.E. Kennedy.

In *"L'Ours Teddy"* the Teddy Bear, dressed in boy's clothing, is joined by an English black character doll, called a "Golliwogg," in a series of adventures, including going to school, having a picnic and playing on the beach.

In *"Le Petit Negre Bambo"* the Teddy Bear is dressed as a girl. In this story the Golliwogg and Teddy take a train journey to the country where they pitch hay, swim in a pond and gather eggs.

The other titles in this series are *"Au Pays Des Betes"* and *"Le Cirque De L'Ours Teddy."*

And how did you like the story of
"Quacky Doodles Meets Danny Daddles")

QUACKY DOODLES
DANNY DADDLES
AND
OLD TEDDY BEAR

"Of course I was glad to console Little Tim,
But I sometimes grew lonely, just playing with him."
"Twas a long time before he recovered, and then,
I was glad I could live in the Toy Box again."
"But the doctor said, first I must surely be steamed,
'Twas a fate of which, truly, I never had dreamed."

"Then over the boiler they placed me—Oh, well!
'Tis a sad tale, but true, in the water I fell!"
"So I lay there, all soaking, like clothes that are soiled,
They intended to steam me, but here I was, boiled!"
"And when it was over—alas! what a sight!
I was soggy and dripping and looked like a fright."

A favorite of collectors, the "Quacky Doodles and Danny Daddles Book," written by Rose Strong Hubbell and illustrated by Johnny Gruelle tells six stories of the adventures of the toy box toys that belong to Tim, Dolly and Dee.

Published in 1916 by P.F. Volland and Company of Chicago, Illinois, the story has an "Old Teddy...wobbly and wrinkly and worn" and a new teddy that is curious about the old teddy's condition.

The old Teddy tells the story one night of being the sole playmate to the young boy Tim during a bout of measles and whooping cough. Under the doctor's orders, to remove all germs, the old Teddy was to be steamed. Precariously hung over a pot of boiling water, the old bear fell in. As the old bear hung on the clothes line blowing in the wind, he was sure he would never be loved again. "But of all the nice toys, as you doubtless have guessed, old Teddy is loved by the children the best."

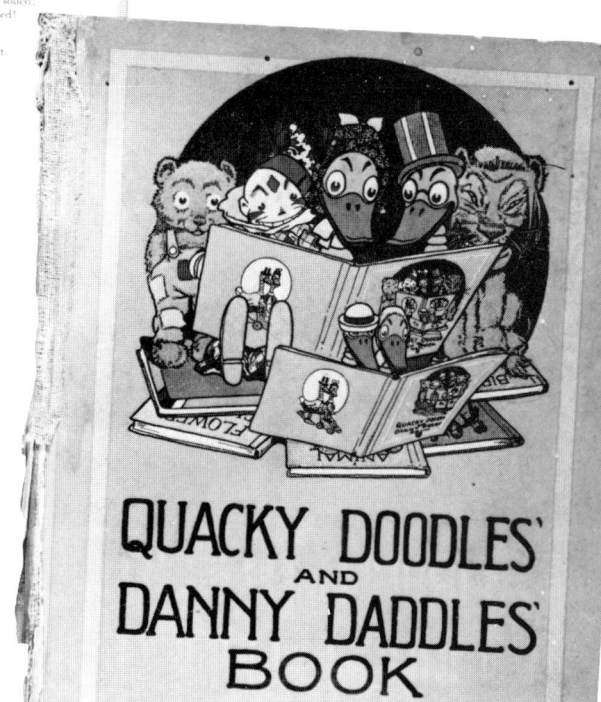

Conclusion

Even though the actual creator of the Teddy Bear as a toy is in dispute — some attribute its creation to Morris Michtom, founder of the Ideal Toy Corporation of America, while others say it was Richard Steiff of the German firm of Steiff — one thing is certain — the Teddy Bear has remained an international symbol of security for nearly a century.

Within a very short time after Clifford Berryman's famous Teddy and his bear cartoon appeared, Teddy Bears were on sale everywhere. Creative business-minded persons quickly picked up on the appeal of the Teddy Bear by producing books, post cards, valentines, playing cards and songs using the word Teddy Bear in the title.

While the original Teddy Bears are quickly snapped up in the antique marketplace little attention has been paid to related Teddy memorabilia. It offers many rewarding images created by outstanding artists.

Index

Note: Each entry below has page numbers indicated in regular type and **illustration** numbers indicated in **bold**.

"Adventures of Molly and Teddy" post cards, 35, **160-165**
Adventures of the Traveling Bears, The, 8
American Post Card Company, 80, **454**
Atwell, Mabel Lucie, 25, **98, 99**
Au Pays Des Betes, 123
Austin, J.I., 38, 122, **184-196**
Bailey, Bill & Corrine, 101, **523**
Barnes, C., 16, 17, **48-50**
Barse & Hopkins, 8, **3**
Barton & Spooner, 31
Bear Detectives, The, 7
Berryman, Clifford K., 6, 16, 125, **46, 47**
Big Teddy, 122
Billy Possum (see Possum, Billy)
BKWI Publishers, 50, **273-300**
Bobbs-Merrill Co., 121
Book plates, **568, 569**
Books, 7, 8, 121-124, **2, 3, 556, 577-583**
Bratton, John W., 108, **546, 547**
Bray, John Randolph, 121, 122
Brundage, Francis, 26, **100-102**
Buchan's Soap, 23, **86-91**
Buckhan, Stephen T., 49, **267-272**
Busy Bear post cards, 31, 38, **184-196**
Busy Bears, The, 38,122
Campbell, V. Floyd, 7, 11, **2, 5-20**
Can label, **551**
Cavally, Frederick L., Jr., 33, 121, **144-159**
Cavally post cards, 33, **144-159**
Cigarette card, **552**
Clapsaddle, Ellen Hattie, 26, **103-106**
Clark, Rose, 48, **255-266**
Colby, Eleanor, 107, **536**
Colombo, 27, **107**
Cracker Jack Bears, 20, 21, **65-80**

Craddock, J.C., 122
"Crane Bears" post cards, 53, **301-307**
Crite, 17, 18, **58**
Culver, R.K., 7, 12, 15, **21-36, 41-46**
Davis, 105
"Days of the Week Bears" post cards, 40, 73, **197-202**
Denslow, W.W., 22, **81-84**
Die cuts, **550, 554, 555, 557, back cover**
Drayton, Grace, 25, 27, 28, 103, 105, 113, **108, 525-534, 556**
Drayton paper dolls, 103-106, **525-534**
Druck Verlag von B. Dondorf, 41, **204-209**
Eaton, Seymour, 6, 7, 11
Ebner, Pauli, 27, **109, 110**
Ellam, W.H., 25, 27, 41, 42, 43, **204-228**
Father Tuck's Toy Rockers, 79, 116, **451-453**
Faulkner, 41
Fisher, Harrison, 27, **111, 112**
Gabriel, Samuel, 26
Gaines, T.R., 16, 17, **48-50**
Gale, Norman, 116
Garman, R.H., 122
Garre, Samuel, 26
Gassaway, Katherine, 28, **113-115**
Gebbie, Grace (see Drayton, Grace)
Gibson Art Co., 31
Gorman, R.H., 78, **450**
Greiner, Magnus, 35, **160-165**
Gross, Edward Publishing, 30
Gruelle, Johnny, 124, **583**
Gulick, L., 18
Gunn, George W., 38, 122, **184**
Gutmann, Bessie Pease, 28, **116**
Hammon, V.O., 73
Hays, Margaret, 28, 103, **117**

Heal, William S., 46, 73, **238-243**
Hildebrand, Fritz, 25, 36, **166-171**
Hillson, D., 54, **308-314**
Holden, Queen, 92-99, **512-521**
"Hold-to-light" post cards, 80, **455-456**
Hubbell, Rose Strong, 124, **583**
Huld, Franz Publishing Co., 17, 77, **51, 446-449**
Ideal Book Builders, 78, **450**
Ideal Toy Corporation of America, 125
Illustrated Post Card Co., 31
Installment post card set, 77, **446-449**
International Art Company, 26, 31, 35, **160-165**
Ives, Sarah Noble, 122
"Jamestown Exposition" post card, 78, **450**
Jewett, Howard, 122
Johnson, Laura Rinkle, 122
Kennedy, A.E., 123
Kennedy, Jimmy, 108
Langsdorff & Co., 55, **320-328**
Latham, Rose, (see O'Neill, Rose)
Leather post cards, 73
Le Cirque De L'Ours Teddy, 123
Lee, Ella Dolbear, 107, **537**
Le Petit Negre Bambo, 123, **582**
Lester Book & Stationery Company, 17
Linn, W.M. & Sons, 17
Little Teddy, 122
Little Toy Bearkins, The, 122
Lounsbury, Fred, 18
L'Ours Teddy, 123, **581**
Magazine Covers, **572-575**
Magazine Illustrations, **570-571**
McGill, Don, 55, **315-319**
McLoughlin Brother, 122
Michtom, Morris, 125

Note: Each entry below has page numbers indicated in regular type and **illustration** numbers indicated in **bold**.

"Molly & Teddy" post cards, 35, **160-165**
More About Teddy B & Teddy G, The Roosevelt Bears, 3, 7, 12
Moreland, B.E., 20, **65-80**
Morgan Importing Company, 19, **62, 63**
Mother Goose's Teddy Bears, 121
Moving Picture Teddies, The, 122
Music (see Sheet Music)
Nathan, M.M., 123
National Art Company, 28, 30, 109, **131, 132, 544**
Novelty Company of Rhode Island, 16
Nystrom, Jenny, 28, **118**
O'Neill, Rose, 25
Ottmann, J. Lithography Co., 46, 90, **245-254, 511**
Pankhurst, Christabel, 18
Paper doll post card, 75, **442**
Paper dolls, 89-107, 510
Periolat, M., 18
Pillard, 25
Piper, Paul, (see Eaton, Seymor)
Playing Cards, 120, **576**
Political post cards, 16-18, **46-61**
Possum, Billy, 17, 18, **54-58**
Providence Novelty Company, 16, **48, 49**
Quacky Doodles & Danny Daddles Book, 124, **583**
Reilly & Britton, 121, **577-579**
Reinthal & Newman, 27, 105
Richardson, Agnes, 29, 89, **119-125, 510**
Riquet & Bolichar, **580**
Rockers, 79, 116, 117, **451-453, 564-567**
Rockwell, Norman, 30, **126**
Roosevelt Bear post cards, 9-15, **5-45**
Roosevelt Bears, The, 9, 16, 23, **2-45**
Roosevelt Bears Abroad, The, 7, 15
Roosevelt Bears — Their Travels and Adventures, The, 7, 11, **2**
Roosevelt, Theodore, 6, 16-18, 73, **46-48, 51**
"Rose Clark Bears" post cards, 48, **255-266**
Rotograph Company, 28, 48, **255-266**
Rudolph Brothers, 18
Saalfield Publishing Co., 101, **523**
Schweizer, 105
Scribner, Charles' Sons, 27

Sheet music, 108-110, **539-543, 545-549**
Shirley Temple paper dolls, 101, 102, **523, 524**
Sommers, G., 9
Steiff, 19, 125, **62-64**
Stern, Edward & Co., Inc., 8, 9, 11, **4-20**
Sweeney, William K., 7
Tablet post cards, 75, **441**
Taft, William H., 17, 18, **52, 53, 55**
Teddy B, 6-9, 121, **2-45**
Teddy Bear ABC, The, 122
Teddy Bear Bread, 22, **81-85**
Teddy Bears Come to Life, The, 121
Teddy Bears, The, 122
Teddy Bears at the Circus, The, 121, **579**
"Teddy Bears at Play" post cards, 41, **225-228**
Teddy Bears at School, The, 121
"Teddy Bears at the Seaside" post cards, 41, **219-224**
Teddy Bears in a Smashup, The, 121, **579**
Teddy Bears in Hot Water, The, 121, **579**
Teddy Bears go Fishing, The, 121 **578**
Teddy Bears on a Lark, The, 121
Teddy Bears on a Toboggan, 121, **577**
"Teddy Bears' Picnic," 108, **546, 547**
Teddy G, 6-9, 121, **2-45**
Temple, Shirley, paper dolls, 101, 102, **523, 524**
Thayer Publishing Company, 33, **144-159**
Theile, Arthur, 25, 30, **127-130**
Tower Manufacturing & Novelty Co., 49, **267-272**
Towne, R.D., 121
T.P. & Company, 44, 45, **229-237**
Traveling Bears Across the Sea, The, 8
Traveling Bears at Play, The, 8
Traveling Bear's Birthday, The, 8
Traveling Bear Detectives, The, 8
Traveling Bears in the East and West, The, 8
Traveling Bears in England, The, 8
Traveling Bears in Fairy Land, The, 8, **3**
Traveling Bears in New York, The, 8
Traveling Bears in Outdoor Sports, The, 8

Tuck Little Bears, 36, **172-183**
Tuck, Raphael & Sons, 25, 26, 28, 33, 36, 37, 41, 73, 79, 105, 116, **166-171, 219-228, 453-454, 564-567**
Twelvetrees, Charles, 30, 109, **131, 132, 544**
Ullman Manufacturing Co., 28, 31, 40, 80, **197-202, 454**
Valentines, 114, 115, **558-563**
Valentine Post Card Co., 25, 31
Volland, P.F. & Co., 124
Wain, Louis, 31, **133**
Wall, Bernhardt, 31, 80, **134, 554**
Weiderseim, Grace, (see Drayton, Grace)
Whitman Publishing Co., 92
Wickham, Constance, 123
Williams, Clara Andrews, 122
Wilson, Rose, (see O'Neill, Rose)
Winsch, John O., 32, **138-143**
Wolf Brothers, 26
Wonderful Story of Teddy the Bear, The, 122
Wood, Lawson Clarence, 31, **135-137**
Wrightman, Francis, P., 7
Writing tablets, 9, **4**
Young, Sheila, 107, **535, 538**
Zim, H.G. Company, 53, **301-307**

BIBLIOGRAPHY

Bull, Peter, *A Hug of Teddy Bears,* New York, E.P. Dutton Inc., 1984.

Bull, Peter, *The Teddy Bear Book,* New York, Random House, Inc., 1969.

Greenhouse, Bernard L., *Political Postcards,* 1900-1980, Syracuse, New York, Postcard Press, 1984.

Ryan, Dorothy B., *Picture Postcards in the United States,* 1893-1918, New York, Clarkson N. Potter, Inc., 1976, 1982.

Schoonmaker, Patricia N., *A Collector's History of the Teddy Bear,* Cumberland, Maryland, Hobby House Press, Inc., 1981.

Waring, Phillippa and Peter, *Teddy Bears.* Great Britian, Souvenir Press, 1980. (Under title *In Praise of Teddy Bears*) London, Treasure Press, 1984.

About the Author

Susan Brown Nicholson, a graduate of Iowa State University, has been a contributing editor to many publications on antiques, including "Collectors' Showcase," "Spinning Wheel," "Antique Toy World," and "The Teddy Bear and Friends."

Nicholson, a recognized authority on paper ephemera, has monthly columns in "Barr's News" and the "Postcard Collector." She has provided the values for several sections of each edition of "Warman's Americana and Collectibles" guide and has lectured to the National Association of Dealers of Antiques on rare and expensive post cards.